Praying to the Lord of Life

Homilies on the
collects of the Christian year
according to
The Book of Alternative Services

Herbert O'Driscoll

Anglican Book Centre
Toronto, Canada

1989
Anglican Book Centre
600 Jarvis Street
Toronto, Ontario
Canada M4Y 2J6

Typesetting by Jay Tee Graphics Ltd.

Canadian Cataloguing in Publication Data

O'Driscoll, Herbert, 1928-
  Praying to the Lord of Life

ISBN 0-921846-05-3

1. Collects - Sermons. 2. Anglican Church of
Canada - Liturgy - Sermon. 3. Anglican
Communion - Liturgy - Sermons. 4. Church year
sermons. 5. Sermons, Canadian (English).*
6. Anglican Church of Canada — Sermons. 7. Anglican Communion
— Sermons. I. Title.

BX5615.047P7 1989   264'.036   C89-090668-8

For my mother,
who taught me
the third collect
of evensong.

Contents

Preface

These reflections on the collects of the *Book of Alternative Services* are offered as a resource for various purposes. Unlike the other volumes in the series *Child of Peace, Lord of Life*, these are not notes on a scripture passage. Rather, each one is a short homily or reflection on the text of the collect for that particular week in the liturgical year.

These short reflections may be useful to anyone responsible for preaching or teaching in the life of the church, or to any worshipper. Some examples may be of help. . .

* In a parish where the *BAS* is used at an early service.
* At a mid-week celebration of the Holy Eucharist.
* Excerpts may be used in the parish bulletin.
* Any worshipper might consider using this collection for a few moments of reflection before the Holy Eucharist. Since not everyone will wish to do this, a number might be made available as people enter.
* It might be suggested to Sunday School teachers who miss the Sunday homily that they might use this book. For the parish to give it as a small gift to such a person might be immensely affirming of their service in the parish.
* Men and women who as laypeople lead worship in many congregations, often far from resources, might find useful material here as they try to commend their faith and commitment to others.

Whatever uses are found for these pages, may they bring God glory, contributing to the cause of God's kingdom as it is served by the community of God's people.

Herbert O'Driscoll
Christ Church, Elbow Park,
Calgary, Pentecost 1989

First Sunday of Advent

Almighty God,
give us grace to cast away the works of darkness
and put on the armour of light,
now in the time of this mortal life
in which your Son Jesus Christ
came to us in great humility,
that on the last day,
when he shall come again in his glorious majesty
to judge both the living and the dead,
we may rise to the life immortal;
through him who lives and reigns
with you and the Holy Spirit,
one God, now and for ever.

The opening image of the Christian year is vivid, startling, sobering. One of the famous four statements of the Buddha is, "Life is suffering." Here we are being informed bluntly and directly that life is conflict. Existence is presented to us in terms of zones of light and darkness. It is an existence for which we require defences and the ability and energy to struggle. If we compare the breath we must take to say this "first sentence" of the Christian year to our first breath as new-born children, then both events convey the same reality to us. Life includes an element of struggle, physical and spiritual.

The word *now* rings out. The spiritual struggle cannot be postponed for some distant spiritual time and realm. It takes place now in this mortal life, in the thousand ongoing ordinary things of everyday, in the unrehearsed and seemingly minor decisions we make every hour. To realize this is to understand something all-important. The spiritual struggle of human life does not take place in larger-than-life melodramatic situations but rather in the ordinary and the mundane and the everyday.

But human life is made more than ordinary by virtue of a certain event. By that event human life is transformed. God has come into our lives. There are footsteps on the planet other than ours, footsteps which, because they walked by one lake in one time, are discoverable by any lake in any time. There are hands which, because they healed in the past, can become hands of healing in the present; words which, because they were spoken with power in the past, can be spoken with power in the present. We speak of course of Our Lord Jesus Christ, once come but forever with us.

Even that coming, inexpressibly significant as it was, did not take place in larger-than-life melodramatic terms. He came to us in great humility. He grew in a woman's womb. He lay in a manger. He knew our pain and our depressions. He tasted the joy and disappointments of relationships. Death was his companion.

But we discover a strange and wonderful thing about him. He lived in our past, but he can be found in our present. He is history, but he is our experience. He is remembered but he is also known. Not only this; there is a mysterious reality which also makes him our future and our judge. The way he lived our human life remains forever the ultimate way to live it. His way judges and measures our lesser ways. We find ourselves bringing our stumbling journeys to his shining journey not only for comparison, inspiration, and encouragement, but also for accountability. He surrounds our existence. In our past he is a remembered child and man. In our present he is friend, companion, Lord. In our future he is judge and measurer. No wonder we say in each Eucharist, ''Christ has died, Christ is risen, Christ will come again.'' In that song we repeat this collect throughout the whole Christian year.

We spoke of this mortal life and now we speak of life

immortal. They are not two but one. They do not exist in different spheres or different realities. They are one reality, one road, one way. The road to immortality begins in the familiar things of this very day. Thanks be to God.

Second Sunday of Advent

Almighty God,
who sent your servant John the Baptist
to prepare your people to welcome the Messiah,
inspire us, the ministers and stewards of your truth,
to turn our disobedient hearts to you,
that when the Christ shall come again to be our judge,
we may stand with confidence before his glory;
who is alive and reigns with you and the Holy Spirit,
one God, now and for ever.

In recent years those who study human dreaming have suggested that the figures appearing in our dreams may be facets of ourselves. This is not a bad way to approach holy scripture. We encounter an exotic tragic figure in John the baptizer, as he was called. We might apply to ourselves the fact that John is identified by what he was seen to do. In that sense, what is your name and mine? Not of course our official name which we write unnumbered times, but the name that others perhaps unconsciously attach to us because of what we do, the things which are essential to our lives and most communicate to others the reality of the man or woman we truly are. Is our name followed in the minds of others by phrases such as the faithful, the carer, the helper; or the deceiver, the neglecter, the hurter.

Thus we meet John in this collect. In what ways do we meet ourselves? Immediately we hear three things said of John. He is sent by God; he sees himself as God's servant; his task is to prepare for something. Every one of these things can be true of our lives if we so choose. Seeing oneself as sent by God is not in any sense puffing oneself up with self-importance. One is sent by God for a purpose by

virtue of being a baptized Christian! In exactly the same way
we become a servant of God. These are not exercises in self-
inflation. In fact, to forget them or to be unaware of them
is to forget our Christian vocation. John embodies these
things for us. Like the figure in our dreams we need to ask
ourselves, What if this figure seemingly outside us is really
an aspect of ourselves?

We live in a civilization where there can sometimes be
a sense of meaninglessness and powerlessness in our
human lives. We wonder why we exist. We can feel irrele-
vant and ineffective. Such feelings can issue in deep depression and even suicide. But to realize our baptism and its
vocation is to possess a weapon to fight such spiritual enemies. To look in the mirror, facing the reality of who we
are — our ordinariness, our pathetic mingling of gifts and
weaknesses — is a salutary exercise. But as we stand there
taking stock, we hear a prayer reminding us that we are
the material which the infinitely gracious and loving God
uses for purposes beyond our understanding. Also as we
look at ourselves, we might remember that what we see is
precisely the imperfect human nature which Our Lord took
upon himself and transformed and lifted to the heights.

We might ask in what sense we could possibly be sent
to prepare people to welcome the Messiah? But every Christian man or woman, if only by their daily quality of life,
is preparing for the Messiah. Consider our relationships
with those nearest to us. What of Christ is in those relationships? What of our efforts to let ourselves, even in the
simplest and most groping ways, become vessels of the will
of Our Lord? What of our attempts to speak haltingly to
our children, or to a friend in an intimate moment, about
the faith which is important to us? What of our efforts to
share in the task of forming a Christian community, group,
or congregation — frustrating and disappointing though that
can sometimes be? Once again we must be ready to grasp
language such as ''prepare your people'' in terms of the
everyday and the accessible. Such language is not for remote

spiritual giants. We in our ordinariness are "the ministers and stewards" of the truth of Christ. By a wonderful and ironic paradox, we are also the ones who have to wrestle with having "disobedient hearts" which need to be turned back to Our Lord! Thanks be to God!

Third Sunday of Advent

God of power and mercy,
you call us once again
to celebrate the coming of your Son.
Remove those things which hinder love of you,
that when he comes,
he may find us waiting in awe and wonder
for him who lives and reigns with you and the Holy Spirit,
one God, now and for ever.

This prayer is an ideal example of how the familiarity of religious language dulls our sense of wonder at what is being said. We say "God of power," and the words are gone almost as they are pronounced. There is no time for images of power to ignite in our imagination. Not all the images of creation would exhaust what we say in those words. Not all the wonder and beauty of the planet, not even the surrounding system of planets or the unimaginable wheeling of the galaxy and its myriad companions in the universe, would exhaust these three small words.

The even greater wonder is that we dare to say we are addressed by this creator God. We say that we are "called." Implicit in this deceptively simple statement is our belief that there is a relationship between our pitiable humanity and the very source of creation. We believe there can even be dialogue between creature and creator. It is either our greatest insight or our greatest delusion.

We dare all this because of a property of God other than power. We name it "mercy." A measure of the mystery of this property is the fact that it is almost impossible to find a synonym for the word. Mercy is not pity or kindness or forgiveness, although every one of these properties can be

found in it. It is all of them and more. It involves the giving of self to another for the sole reason that one wishes
and longs to. It matters not that the other is unimaginably
lesser, as is our humanity before God. The gift of God's
self is still given. The ultimate self-giving is in the One who
comes. No wonder we think in these weeks of our being
called to a celebration.

As the words *God of power* call for all our powers to con-
ceive the infinite beauty and wonder and terror of creation,
so the words *coming of your Son* call us to contemplate this
mystery at the heart of Christian faith. I am about to witness infinite power choosing a way of weakness, invulner-
ability making itself vulnerable, divinity entering into
humanity. The fact that we sometimes have difficulty accepting this should reassure us. If it did not take considerable
effort on our part to believe this, it would be a measure of
the shallowness, glibness, and thoughtlessness of our
spirituality! When we begin to find incarnation readily
acceptable, it should come as a warning to us.

Our petition is a request to God to remove those things
which hinder our love of God. What an immense task we
give to God! Each of us has only to consider in silence for
a few minutes those things which hinder our love of God,
to realize what we ask. In that silence we are not by any
means thinking only of wrong or unworthy things. We have
to think also of the finest and most precious and most worthwhile things in our lives! Our loving of those nearest and
dearest to us. Our perfectly legitimate ambitions to achieve
this or that. The myriad private projects we wish to carry
out.

None is an ultimate direction or focus for my life. None
is a light in itself to be followed. Every single one shines
with a reflected light. My task is not to be mesmerized by
the consuming interest of the task or project or relationship
in itself, but to see beyond and within it the presence and
the grace of God. The moment I do that, the moment I offer
these perfectly valid aspects of my life, a mysterious thing

happens. I am given them back. I can pursue them freely, because they have now been hallowed. Once I have realized this, my life becomes ''a waiting in awe and wonder'' for the God who comes, not merely in a Christ of history but in the Christ who can be my daily companion in all I do. Thanks be to God.

Fourth Sunday of Advent

Heavenly Father,
who chose the Virgin Mary, full of grace,
to be the mother of our Lord and Saviour,
now fill us with your grace,
that we in all things may embrace your will
and with her rejoice in your salvation;
through Jesus Christ our Lord,
who lives and reigns with you and the Holy Spirit,
one God, now and for ever.

If we could meet Mary in her time and place, we would see a young woman much like many young women of that time and place. We would not see some detached shining figure, suitably haloed for our adoration. Mary, like the rest of us, was a human being. Human beings are the material God has to work with. That statement is not merely stating the obvious. It should give us hope and joy because it means that we are the material by which God forms the world.

All through the Bible there is a recurring event. When God wishes to do something, the first thing that God does is to find a human being to carry out that particular purpose. Abraham and Sarah are found to begin a people, Noah and his family to open a future, Moses to lead a people — on and on the pattern goes. All of these people would express total astonishment at the idea that they might be special or extraordinary in any way. In fact, in every case the scriptures reveal their human weaknesses. Yet they were chosen to be the instruments of God for God's purposes.

But the question remains, Why were they chosen? The final answer lies hidden in the inscrutable ways of God, but of one thing we can be sure. They had some gifts which God saw to be useful for the task in hand. To say that they were all, including Mary, mere human beings is not to deny that they embodied gifts and abilities and strengths which God discerned within them and decided to draw out. Those gifts within us all we call by the lovely word *grace*.

We say that Mary was full of grace. It is difficult to find other words for that. Perhaps it means that Mary possessed the spiritual material from which God would make possible what is almost inconceivable. Human though she was, God would use Mary's being to enter not merely her humanity but the humanity of us all.

But here we come to the heart of this collect. To enter into humanity is precisely, but in a lesser sense, what God wishes to do through every single one of us. That is why we now move from Mary to ourselves. We ask to be filled with grace. First of all we ask because we realize how empty we sometimes feel. We say *feel* not *are*. That is important. We may feel empty of grace, but God is always waiting to fill the seeming emptiness with the inexhaustible grace which is the nature of God.

We ask grace "to embrace God's will." This is not a mere spiritual ideal. Our embracing of God's will can begin the moment we acknowledge the claim of a higher will than our own. Jesus once said that he was come "not to do mine own will but the will of him that sent me." That is really the goal of any Christian's life. We cannot live that perfectly, but when we fail we can accept pardon and begin again.

Finally we want to "rejoice in God's salvation." To be a Christian gives us a gift beyond price. It tells us who we are and what our lives are for. We are of God and for God and the pattern of being that is Our Lord. Millions of people would give a great deal to possess that sense of identity and purpose in their lives. It is ours by baptism. It is Our Lord's gift to us. And he is Mary's gift to us. Thanks be to God.

Christmas — at Midnight

Eternal God,
this holy night is radiant
with the brilliance of your one true light.
As we have known
the revelation of that light on earth,
bring us to see the splendour of your heavenly glory;
through Jesus Christ our Lord,
who is alive and reigns with you and the Holy Spirit
one God, now and for ever.

Once in the North Atlantic late at night, I watched a flare sent aloft to explode in the vault of the sky. We were standing on deck, looking out toward the coast of Newfoundland but seeing nothing because of the darkness. Suddenly the flare blazed out high above us. Light poured in all directions, creating a vast dome which became our world for a few precious beautiful seconds. We were in no danger. The firing of the flare was merely a training exercise. Yet when the flare created that world of light, it brought forth all sorts of feelings. For a few moments it showed us where we were. It showed the direction in which the great swells were moving. It showed us our own faces upturned and wondering, greedy for the light. It pushed out the boundaries of our vision, formerly imprisoned by the darkness of a moonless night. The few moments of light gave a sense of recovered freedom, of reassurance, of confidence. When the last of the light died, the darkness rushed back and claimed the whole world.

This night is like that, and the first sentence of this collect captures its glory in a single brilliant image. There is indeed a kind of radiance about this night. It matters not whether we are in a country church or in a great cathedral; an effort has been made to push back the boundaries of the ordinary and the everyday. There are lights not usually here, perhaps the candles of an Advent Wreath or the extra candles brought out for special occasions, the star placed by willing hands over the altar or the lights on a tree. Tonight time is not ordinary. Time and night and dawn and day are lit by a radiance that, however simple, makes them all sacred time, and the sacredness of this time is in the fact that all our lesser lights are reflections of the great light of the Child.

But seeing the light on one particular night is not enough. That is the tragedy for many. A religion of one night, however lovely and shining it may be, is mere sentimentality. I remember on that long-ago night, immediately after the light of the flare died, that the engines of the ship rose in power as a new direction was chosen, the ocean was challenged, and the next stage of our journey began. This night has to be like that if it is to be of spiritual significance for us. It is not enough to come to the manger; one must turn from it. And then, accepting what the occupant of the manger means, one must begin to live out that meaning, choosing what may be new directions, challenging previous ways and assumptions, continuing the journey of one's life with the knowledge that something has changed.

The collect says that we need to know the "revelation" of the lights of this night. The lights themselves are only pointers to another reality. The lights in the church or in the shopping centre, the lights of homeward-bound cars or a group of carol singers, the lights on a neighbour's tree or our own porch welcoming us home — all are in themselves less than the truth of this night. They serve only to light us toward the truth of the Child and what the Child must become in our lives. The lights exist only to "bring us to see" something else. If in this child of simplicity and poverty and vulnerability the creator God of the universe lies embodied, then we can find that same God in the sim-

plicity and poverty and vulnerability of our lives, our relationships, and our society. If this insight comes to us, then,
even though it is sadly obvious that earth is not heaven,
nevertheless heaven lies hidden in the things of earth.
Thanks be to God.

First Sunday after Christmas

Almighty God,
you have shed upon us the new light
of your incarnate Word.
May this light, enkindled in our hearts,
shine forth in our lives;
through Jesus Christ our Lord,
who lives and reigns with you,
in the unity of the Holy Spirit,
one God, now and for ever.

I have often thought of the essential difference between the way our culture carries out its celebrations and the ancient way of Christian experience. By and large in our society celebrations last only a short time and are then totally finished. We might apply this to the phenomenon we know today as Christmas. But we need to differentiate between the social phenomenon and the reality of the Christian feast.

In our society the celebration of Christmas gathers to a crescendo over preceding weeks, culminates in a single day's family gathering, and then ends. That ending is instantaneous. The public media reverts to its normal pattern of programming; the stores return to their normal business; the stillness of the streets is shattered. Contrast this with the form of the Christian liturgical year. It speaks to us of preparation for the weeks before. The pressure of our culture tries to transform that preparation into celebration, and to a large extent that pressure has succeeded. The day itself, as is the day in the general culture, is one of celebration. But there the similarity ends. Because then we Christians are offered a long period of reflection to savour the joy of this event, to linger over its loveliness, to think of its meaning, to turn it around and around as we would a many-faceted jewel, looking now at this truth, now at that.

That is precisely what we hear in this collect, and, indeed, will hear for the next few weeks. We will be turning the jewel of this season, looking deep into its truths and its glories. As we do so, radiant beams shine out of it and light up our searching hearts and minds.

"The new light of your incarnate Word." We have almost forgotten the newness of this event we call the Incarnation. What is new is that God is among us. Even this statement smothers under our familiarity with it. It is not saying that faith in God is among us, or that the longing for God is among us — all of which is very true. It is taking one giant step beyond those statements by saying that God is now among us! Once again we might take comfort from the difficulty we have in assimilating the wonder of this. There is a verse in the Psalms that says, "Such knowledge is too wonderful and excellent for me. I cannot attain unto it." The fact that we find it so difficult to comprehend is perhaps the measure of the mystery.

Perhaps *comprehend* is the wrong kind of word. In itself it is certainly incomplete. Comprehension with the mind is only the first step to assimilating the light of Christ into our lives. That is where the collect takes us next. Christian faith is never a matter of merely knowing. There is a demand concerning what we do with our new knowing. It is necessary that the light of Our Lord's birth illuminate our minds. It is necessary, but it is not of itself sufficient. Something which has begun must go much further. The light must take two more steps within us. From being grasped by our thinking it must be experienced in our feeling, and finally it must become real in our acting. "Enkindled in our hearts" it must then "shine forth in our lives."

The truth is that the word *incarnation* says it all without the help of any other language. Christ in flesh, Christ in the mind, Christ in the heart, Christ in the action. Thanks be to God.

The Naming of Jesus

Eternal Father,
we give thanks for your incarnate Son,
whose name is our salvation.
Plant in every heart, we pray,
the love of him who is the Saviour of the world,
our Lord Jesus Christ;
who lives and reigns with you and the Holy Spirit,
one God, in glory everlasting.

Thomas Stearns Eliot, that great Christian poet of this century, near the beginning of his poem cycle *Old Possum's Book of Practical Cats*, has a piece called "The Naming of Cats." With tongue-in-cheek seriousness he tells us how important this naming is among cats, how each cat has three names, each of which possesses an ever-increasing level of significance. Naming among cats is obviously not casual or incidental.

In a family the naming of a child is likewise not casual. Probably the process differs from family to family. Sometimes the name of the coming child is easily decided on. For some reason everyone agrees what it should be. But in other families much time and thought and care is given.

Naming is a very mysterious thing. We notice how many people own up to having problems with their name. They try to change it, using different forms of it in different stages of life, or adapting it if they move into a new place. Many people have a middle name they keep hidden, or smile shyly at when it is revealed. Names are significant, powerful, and mysterious.

This is especially so with the name of Jesus. We can no longer regard that name as any other name. It has become uniquely appropriated by the one who used it and lived with it and responded to it. Even when it is used inappropriately as an oath, it receives a kind of back-handed compliment to its significance and undying power.

For a Christian, so this collect tells us, the name of Jesus is salvation. That is an enormous statement. Notice what it does not say. The name of Jesus does not tell us about or promise us salvation. The name of Jesus *is* our salvation. That fact has been true in unnumbered lives. Christian history is replete with the experiences of those for whom this name has been a mysterious power. Today many Christians use Our Lord's name as a mantra, repeated slowly and lovingly in a time of meditation, invoking in oneself a sense of his presence. Many men and women going through some extremely demanding experience, one which threatens to break their nerve or exhaust their own resources, find new resolve by the quiet saying of the name of Jesus.

There are aspects of Christian spiritual formation which we have in recent generations neglected. Perhaps it is because we felt they would somehow take care of themselves, or that a vaguely Christian society would provide support for their survival. We have been quite wrong. One such aspect is the use of what has for centuries been called the Holy Name.

We live at a time when many Christian families are struggling to find ways in which parents can communicate to their children the elements of Christian faith. As they do this, most men and women feel the lack of sufficient knowledge of the faith in themselves. Much of this feeling of inadequacy is unnecessary. There are simple but infinitely valuable and powerful ways in which parents can communicate their reverence and their commitment to Christ. One simple way is to inculcate a sense of the sacredness of the name of Jesus Our Lord. It can be made clear in simple and gentle ways that for us in our family this word is unlike any other word. This word is the name of the most important person in the world to us. This word is the name of the person we follow. This word is holy. Thanks be to God.

Second Sunday of Christmas

God of power and life,
the glory of all who believe in you,
fill the world with your splendour
and show the nations the light of your truth;
through Jesus Christ your Son our Lord,
who is alive and reigns with you and the Holy Spirit,
one God, now and for ever.

Because of recent explorations in interplanetary space, we know that when we reach the edge of our solar system we will look back at the Sun and see only a faint yellow source of light and warmth. That light and warmth affects the outer planets only minimally.

We are now moving out in time from the birth of Our Lord as celebrated in the Christmas feast. We too are looking back, as time takes us away from the carols and the lights and the music and the family gathering. But unlike our journeying from the Sun, we are not moving away from the spiritual light and warmth of that event. We find that as Christians we cannot. The light of Christ did not blaze in a particular history only to be fastened into the prison of that history. Nor is the light of Christ so strong that it pours across the centuries and illuminates our own time. It does indeed do that, but not in that way. The light of Christ illuminates our day because it lives and radiates in our day. It is not just a splendid and beautiful memory but a contemporary reality.

Notice how no collect begins with such words as "God of our great tradition" or "God of the unchanging past." The opening words of this collect, "God of power and life," are pulsating with nowness, contemporaneity, life. They are our response to the name we know God claims — I AM.

We say the same of Our Lord a few sentences later. He "is alive and reigns." This collect is infused with a sense of the living God and the living Christ, with emphasis on the living, the palpable aliveness of both. Again, we are not travelling away from past and fixed realities, each growing weaker with the passage of time and generations, each demanding greater use of our memories. We do not say that this God is the wonderful memory of those who believe. We say in this collect that "God is the glory of all who believe."

What does language like that mean? How can God be my glory? That word *glory* is vast and many faceted. We might take a line such as "In the cross of Christ I glory" to see if it helps. To glory in something means to take immense joy from it, to regard it as a source of satisfaction and energy, to think of it as a powerful resource in one's life, to see meaning in it, and to receive inspiration from it. All of this is what we mean by saying that God is our glory.

But then we take a quantum leap. We move out beyond our personal relationship with Our Lord and we try to express a much larger vision, that of a world filled with the moral splendour of Christ. We try to envision that splendour in terms of a society of peace and justice. We go even further. In our prayer, "show the nations the light of your truth," we envision a world of changed relationships. This prayer is not one of mere Christian imperialism. We do not pray that the whole world will necessarily become Christian in our own terms. We pray that all that is of Christ may find its dwelling in the lives of all nations and cultures. For them, that may be named in ways other than we name it, but the reality which both they and we discern in Christ will be the same glorious reality.

As we pray this, we might remind ourselves that the first voice to pray in this way for the newly conceived Christ Child was his mother Mary, when she sang Magnificat. Thanks be to God.

The Epiphany

Eternal God,
who by a star
led wise men to the worship of your Son.
Guide by your light the nations of the earth,
that the whole world may know your glory;
through Jesus Christ our Lord,
who lives and reigns with you and the Holy Spirit,
one God, now and for ever.

Every year in newspapers across the country articles appear during the Christmas and Epiphany season which claim to tell us the truth behind the story of the star of the Magi. Always in these articles the word *really* is prominent. They are, they claim, telling us what really happened, what was really behind the mythical event, what we really can believe. The implication, intended or otherwise, seems to be that in the story of the wise men there exists something less than a reality. Ironically there exists in the story a reality and a truth at least as significant, and in certain ways far more significant, than the ceaseless searching for precise astronomical information.

"Eternal God," begins the collect, "who by a star led wise men to the worship of your Son." These mysterious visitors are now well known to us as figures of the life of Persia. They were men of intellect and sophistication who gave us the insights of early astronomy, and because they sought to link their astronomical data with the lives of persons and of societies, they also gave us what we have come to call astrology. This ancient searching for insight into the meaning of human life has been proved to be remarkably resilient down through the centuries. I write in a year when western society is still both amused and appalled that the most powerful figure in the western world has admitted governing his calendar by astrological prediction. For that matter, so do millions of Christians. If challenged, most would plead that their interest in astrology is an amusing diversion. Nevertheless the practice remains widespread. So perhaps it is important to realize that the opening words of this collect are not so much emphasizing that the wise men were led by a star, but that they were led to the worship of the Son of God. It is because of this latter fact that Christian tradition accords them wisdom and discernment. For a Christian, the search for reality is not in terms of discovering the patterns in the night sky at that time. A Christian seeks to find as a living reality in his or her life what the Magi found to be a reality for them. The reality for them was the discovery of the Child. Whatever the movements of the stars may have been was a means to that overriding reality rather than any end in itself.

We ask God to ''guide by your light the nations of the earth.'' An ancient tradition speaks of three wise men, one from each of the three great continents known to the ancient world. The tradition pointed to the universal significance of the birth of this Child. The collect hints at this meaning to extend the Christian hope beyond the individual. That hope is also for the societies in which we individuals live and beyond, for the totality of humanity in which those societies exist. That hope, as expressed here, is ''that the whole world may know your glory.''

Such language is not vague out of weakness but out of the difficulty of even expressing the vast extent of such a vision. We are all like Paul, when in the eighth chapter of his letter to the Romans he tries to encompass a vision of personal, social, and world transformation so vast as to be almost impossible to articulate. In spite of this Paul tries, as we must continue to try.

This feast of the Epiphany and that of the Ascension

have in common the purpose of extending our Christian vision beyond any limitations we would place on it. In both feasts we are shown the whole planet as the potential domain of what we have glimpsed in Jesus Christ. Thanks be to God.

The Baptism of the Lord

Eternal Father,
who at the baptism of Jesus
revealed him to be your Son,
anointing him with the Holy Spirit,
keep your children, born of water and the Spirit,
faithful to their calling;
through Jesus Christ our Lord,
who lives and reigns with you and the Holy Spirit,
one God, now and for ever.

Nowhere in the life of Our Lord does a literal understanding of scripture so obviously deprive us of spiritual benefits as in our reading of his baptism. Nowhere is it more necessary for us to grasp the meaning of scripture as we ourselves try to wrestle with our own identity as baptized Christians.

Our Lord is about thirty. His life up to this point, we must presume, has pursued the normal patterns of a man of his time and society. He must have experienced some inner wrestling as the call of the Father became stronger and more defined. For all we know, there may have been directions tried which proved unsatisfactory, and from which he retreated to wait for further response to the praying he so obviously did with regularity and devotion. Such efforts are our own experience, with their frustrations and disappointments.

However, there comes a call which refuses to be denied. He is impelled to go south to John's preaching. We do not know what effort that departure entailed. If the other evidence of family responses is any indication, he may have left in the face of opposition. Religious movements were many and varied in that society and time. His motive may well have been strongly questioned by friends and family. He may have felt a weight of responsibility as an earner and provider. We do not know, but such issues were possible. He leaves for the encounter which will change him forever.

In the brown waters of the Jordan he feels the water devour him. Light dims, breath stops, symbolically life for a moment ends. Then there is the sun again, warmth again, breath again, life again. At this moment, the gospel writer tells us, the voice comes. "Eternal Father," says the collect, "who at the baptism of Jesus revealed him to be your Son." Revealed him to whom? Primarily it would seem to himself. When that happens the dove comes, alighting upon Jesus.

How tragic if we fasten this into the prison of the literal. If we do, we are saying that certain things are possible in a long-ago time and in special circumstances which are not possible now. We do not expect voices from the sky, nor do we expect doves to alight at moments in contemporary spiritual journeying. Yet it is essential that we ask what the voice and the dove were then, and therefore what they are always in the mysterious ways of God and as the mysterious instruments God chooses.

To speak in this way and to appeal for such thinking is not one whit to lessen God's presence and glory in this matter. It is merely to release them into present and future Christian experience. Surely the voice which proclaims Jesus as Son can be heard by us at a like moment in our spiritual journey. The second half of the collect is praying for this very gift. If I set out from my "Nazareth" of home and familiarity in genuine search for what God's will may be for me, in genuine intention to offer my life to God, surely my self-offering will be rewarded by a deep sense of affirmation, a sense of being named by God as son or daughter. And, should this happen, then just as surely there will come inner peace and joy which are the true gifts of the Spirit. In that moment the dove in very truth comes to me.

I will seek for language, as all before and after me have done and will do. The language of the collect speaks of being ''born of water and the spirit.'' This then is our prayer for new birth and for grace to live faithfully the new life given to us. Thanks be to God.

Second Sunday after Epiphany, Proper 2

Almighty God,
your Son our Saviour Jesus Christ
is the light of the world.
May your people,
illumined by your word and sacraments,
shine with the radiance of his glory,
that he may be known, worshipped, and obeyed
to the ends of the earth;
who lives and reigns with you and the Holy Spirit
one God, now and for ever.

Light is the predominant symbol in the expression of Christian faith. The New Testament uses it often, beginning in the gospels themselves. Light blazes in the heavens at Our Lord's birth. It emanates from him at his transfiguration. Shining figures appear in the time of his ascension. He himself speaks of his being Light, of his having come that we may have light. For John it is a constant symbol challenging the darkness. Paul is confronted on the Damascus road by a blaze of light. Through the letters of the early church and into the Revelation, light continues to be used as the symbol of Christ. From the blazing vivid art of Byzantium, light cascades down mosaic and dome, and on through time and the centuries to this collect and its ancient statement that ''Jesus Christ is the light of the world.''

When we come to a statement like this, we can pause and quietly think about the innumerable lips and voices that have said these words. Generations of men and women engaged in their own spiritual journey as we are, sometimes struggling in personal darkness as we do, have said this statement to themselves. They have not only said it; they have also prayed it silently, have sung it in praise, and have reflected upon it in contemplation. A statement such as this comes down to us as an indescribably precious gift, a kind of heirloom of a vast family who has now decided to entrust it to us for safe keeping and faithful use.

''May your people, illumined by your word and sacraments, shine with the radiance of his glory.'' Very often those involved in the healing ministry will suggest that as we lift someone in prayer for healing, we might deliberately image them as being within a pool of shining light, this light being the outpouring love of God. This is what we are being asked by the collect to do for others in this moment. We are being asked to image ourselves as worshipping in a great area of shining light, a light that has as its source the Bible on the lectern and the bread and wine on the altar, those very things which can easily become over familiar and dulled in our perceptions. We are being asked to do this so that we will realize as we look about us that we have all become shining beings, our dullness changed, our ordinariness transformed. We have become for one another ''a people . . . shining with the radiance of his glory.'' How very much this simple act of inspired imagination is needed in so many congregations whose light has become dulled and whose vision has dimmed.

Why is it so necessary to do this? Because Christ can be light only in his people. Our prayer is that we may shine so that ''he may be known, worshipped, and obeyed to the ends of the earth.'' It must be through us that he shines in the world. Putting it mildly, we so often feel anything but shining! We need to realize that we do not have to go to the ends of the earth, because Christ is already there in men and women like us — people who drink the wine with us, break the bread with us, and name with us the same Lord Jesus. We are never given the Christian vision in easily palatable bite sizes! Our Lord never shows us just small

35mm slides of the Christian vision. Always he puts us down in front of a giant 70mm screen and presents us with breathtaking vistas! Why? Because he knows well that left to ourselves we would mess around for ever with those tiny slides, and he just won't let us! Thanks be to God.

Third Sunday after Epiphany, Proper 3

Almighty God,
by grace alone you call us
and accept us in your service.
Strengthen us by your Spirit,
and make us worthy of your call;
through Jesus Christ our Lord,
who lives and reigns with you and the Holy Spirit,
one God, now and for ever.

The first line of this collect holds, slightly disguised, one of the greatest of all insights about Christian faith. Giants of Christian history such as Augustine, Paul, and Luther would immediately be reminded of the insight which under-lay much of their thinking and changed the shape of Chris-tian history.

"By grace alone you call us." What does this mean for my day-to-day living as a Christian? It means that there is something I must realize about my relationship with God. It is something wonderful and deep which is essential to that relationship.

The relationship between a Christian and his or her Lord does not depend on human actions but on divine grace. We need to say more to bring out the most important truth in that statement. Quite obviously my actions do indeed affect my relationship with God. It could not be otherwise. For instance, my actions affect my awareness of that relation-ship. If I turn my will from my Lord's will, then I am con-scious of having distanced myself from his presence. If I cease to pray, to worship, to grow in the knowledge of him, then I damage the relationship given to me at my baptism. But — and here is the whole point of the matter — the relationship itself, once made, is there for ever. We have only to think of the other great relationships of our lives. A person may be a perfectly hopeless son or daughter to a parent, but nothing can change the fact that the relationship exists. On a human level the relationship can die, in the sense of its being no longer active or discernible. Meetings cease, letters and phone calls stop, even thinking about the other can come to an end. But with God the relationship continues as one of deep commitment toward the creature. There need only be the slightest indication on our part that we wish to turn again toward that love and it reaches out, encouraging, attracting, desiring. Our Lord never ceases to offer grace, never ceases to call us. Even the wish to turn again to him is itself a spark of grace given breath by him within us, so that it may in time burst into flame.

"By grace . . . you accept us in your service." Very often we reveal the way we have come to see our relationship with our Lord. We use language such as "going to the church of our choice." We will hear someone say, "Maybe I should check out Christianity some day," as if it were a new kind of product to try. Always the initiative is seen as ours. We are to be in control. We will do God this wonderful favour of giving our time or allegiance or support. Here in the collect we are told the truth. The boot is on the other foot. We do not choose, rather we are chosen. It is we who have received the honour of Our Lord's choosing, not he the honour of our choosing. Our Lord is not grateful for our following him. Gratitude is what we offer to him for calling us to follow!

The collect goes on to remind us that even when Our Lord does call us, he is not compelled by some special quality or superiority he sees in us. Even when we are called, we are not worthy of his call. He still has to make us worthy. He calls us as we are, not as he wishes us to be. He calls us because he sees in us the potential which we ourselves do not see. He calls not so much the person we are as the person we are capable of becoming, helped by his grace. Looking back over this collect we see how the initiative is with God in every stage of the relationship with us. By God we are called. By God we are accepted for service. By God we are strengthened. By God we are made worthy of being called. Thanks be to God.

Fourth Sunday after Epiphany, Proper 4

Living God,
in Christ you make all things new.
Transform the poverty of our nature
by the riches of your grace,
and in the renewal of our lives
make known your glory;
through Jesus Christ our Lord,
who is alive and reigns with you and the Holy Spirit,
one God, now and for ever.

Transformation is a very wonderful thing to see in a human life. Someone unemployed finds a job, and we see them transformed from a kind of deadness to being radiantly alive. We see someone who has been alone for a long time discover a relationship. We see someone who has wrestled with a long illness and at last recovers and goes from strength to strength. In all these we see people undergoing amazing transformation, and we wonder at it and rejoice in it.

Christians believe that the birth, life, death, and resurrection of Jesus Christ has transformed creation. That is an enormous statement. Can we find some ways of getting at its meaning?

The early Christians, particularly those who formed the New Testament, realized they had to think through the meaning of the events which had taken place among them. They knew they had encountered something extraordinary in the person of Our Lord. He had had a transforming effect on their own lives, but was it more than this? Was there something larger being hinted at by the personal experience of transformation they had known. In living a completely new quality of human life, had Jesus in fact made a fundamental change in the quality of creation itself?

The collect says, "Living God, in Christ you make all things new." Can that be true? That is the question they asked and the mystery they wrestled with. We can see moments in their writing when they broke through to further levels of a mysterious transformation. Paul particularly breaks through when he writes to the Christian community in Rome. He says that Christ does not merely respond to the sense of incompleteness we humans have. Christ also is the response to the sense of incompleteness which our whole society has, which even the whole of creation feels. Somehow Christ comes into all those levels and calls them to the fullness and completeness and wholeness which he lived out and communicates.

Perhaps a further way of explaining that is to say that Our Lord himself is our humanity lifted and transformed. He is calling us forward and upward to become what he is. He wishes to "transform the poverty of our human nature." Just as it is said that we use only a small fraction of our brains, it would seem that we use only a small part of our spirits, a poor pathetic fraction. But if we can even start to do that, then by virtue of our own partial transformation, we will begin to transform society. And if we even start to do that, we will begin to transform not only our human relationships but also the relationship of our humanity to the whole of creation. Meanwhile, as we carry out this work of God, we must always remember that everything is from God — the grace felt within us, the vision emerging from that grace, and the energy to work for the realizing of that vision — all come from God's grace working within us.

Our prayer here is that Christ may transform and renew us. Do we really want that? Because if it happens, it will not necessarily be on our terms but on God's terms. We don't know what our transformation and renewal would lead to. In what ways would we wish to be transformed? What particular things in my life do I wish to be renewed? Those are very difficult questions to answer because the very fact that we are within ourselves, that we actually are our selves, makes it impossible for us to see as Our Lord sees us. All we can do is to hand ourselves over to him for his reforming and his renewing. That too is what the collect says. Any transforming will be ''by the riches of his grace,'' any renewing will ''make known his glory.'' Thanks be to God.

Fifth Sunday after Epiphany, Proper 5

Merciful Lord,
grant to your faithful people pardon and peace,
that we may be cleansed from all our sins
and serve you with a quiet mind;
through Jesus Christ our Lord,
who is alive and reigns with you and the Holy Spirit,
one God, now and for ever.

Sometimes we rediscover by the sheer loveliness of a piece of prose or poetry that language can of itself be healing. This lovely old collect is such a piece. It is not an accident that it has for a long time been used in place of an absolution. The very sound of its words are themselves absolving, freeing, reassuring.

We pray for pardon. Perhaps it is even more important to say that we are praying for a sense of being pardoned. Sometimes Christians can have a knowledge of the nature of God as forgiving, but they are unable to appropriate that into their lives. We can know of God's pardoning nature, can be told of it a thousand times, but not be able to apply it to ourselves.

The process whereby we become forgiven people is a double-layered one. We need to become aware that God's gift to us is forgiveness. Then in a mysterious way we need to accept this gift and give it in turn to the part of ourselves which needs it. In other words, it is not enough to know that God forgives me. I need to know in such a way that I am given permission to forgive myself. As is often said, sometimes people have not yet forgiven themselves years after God has long forgiven them!

We pray for peace. That word peace is vast and contains many facets of meaning. We are praying here for personal peace. We are always at war within — war between what we have and what we want, between who we are and who we wish to be, between our battling moods, our different ambitions that cannot all be fulfilled, our desires that cannot all be satisfied. We pray for some resolution of that seething battlefield, for at least some temporary truces in a war zone which will endure as long as we live, its contours and its issues ever changing over the years, but the eternal conflict going on.

But when we pray for both a sense of having been forgiven and accepted and for a sense of inner peace, we are not praying for either of these things as ends in themselves. We often fall into that trap, but this collect corrects the tendency. Here in these lines neither pardon nor peace are ends. They are means to another and more worthy end. We pray for them both so that having received them we can "serve God with a quiet mind."

Another way of expressing this is to say that we are praying that with God's grace in our lives we can lay to rest our own heavy agenda which saps our spiritual energies. For much of our lives we are fighting spiritual civil wars inside ourselves. We are like a country so torn by unrest within itself that it has nothing left to play its part on the world stage. To know that God fully accepts us as we are can be a source of inner peace. Having that inner peace we can get on with the task of offering what we really are to be used by God as God wills.

The collect has a wonderful phrase for this state of being. It speaks of having "a quiet mind." Quiet comes from the Latin "*quietus*." In that sense quiet does not necessarily mean slow or idle or passive or weak, or any of those negative things so feared and despised by our overactive and hypertensive time. Having a quiet mind simply means having a mind that, because it is at peace with God, is thereby willing and able to serve God. Thanks be to God.

Sixth Sunday after Epiphany or between 8 and 14 May, Proper 6

Almighty and everliving God,
whose Son Jesus Christ healed the sick
and restored them to wholeness of life,
look with compassion on the anguish of the world,
and by your power make whole all peoples and nations;
through Jesus Christ our Lord,
who lives and reigns with you and the Holy Spirit,
one God, now and for ever.

Of all the ways in which Our Lord is seen to have acted in the world, the most obvious and universal is his work as a healer. In every one of the gospels there is overall agreement about this. The differences are only in details of particular events. It is quite undeniable that whatever allowance we make for the naming of diseases in those days — for example, the term leprosy covered many skin diseases as we know them — Our Lord quickly became known as one who had the gift of healing. Even when it is quite obvious that he has other purposes as he journeys through an area, it is for this that he will be constantly approached. It is to healing that he gives himself again and again, even when others who care for him try to spare him the drain and weariness of this work.

We have only to think of the episode of Bartimaeus who calls out insistently to Jesus when Our Lord's every thought is toward the dangers and the possible suffering ahead of him in Jerusalem. The disciples try to fend off Bartimaeus, but it is Our Lord who voluntarily turns and asks for the man to be brought, then willingly and generously heals him. It is important to mention these things because they show very clearly the degree to which Our Lord saw his vocation in the world as a healer.

He "restored them to wholeness of life." An essential description of what Our Lord did. We see this very often. A person will come or will be brought to Our Lord for physical healing. Our Lord will intuit that there is something deep seated in the life which is being transposed into physical illness. In our terms those inner forces may be guilt or fear or anxiety or tension. Jesus offers healing at that level of the person's being, so that there may issue healing at the physical level. This is of vital importance for us as we return today in the practice of medicine to an acknowledgement that our humanity is an intricate balance of body, mind, and spirit. All of this subtle and complex reality is contained in Jesus' remark when he has just healed a man brought to him on a pallet by friends. Responding to the astonishment and indignation caused by his forgiving the man's sins, Our Lord asks a question as contemporary for us as the very latest medical paper. He enquires, "Which is easier, to say 'Your sins are forgiven' or to say 'Rise and walk' "? (Matthew 9.5).

Now the collect changes focus. How can there be healing on a level other than the individual in a broken and anguishing world? How can there be a making "whole all peoples and nations"? As Our Lord healed in his earthly lifetime, how can his contemporary body in the world, that body which the church claims to be, become the means of healing in communities and in whole societies.

If we were to ask them, the many voices of what is today being called liberation theology would say to us that this is the very heart of their struggle — to make Jesus Christ the figure who can be a focus of healing and renewed hope in their societies. They would say that by their celebration of the Eucharist they are envisioning a society which has been made whole in terms of the acceptance of all, food and drink for all, justice and peace for all. We in our developed world may search for other ways in which, as the body of Christ, we can pursuade all levels of government to pursue policies and political decisions which reflect in some way the healing and wholeness which Our Lord so obviously wills for all men and women. Thanks be to God.

Seventh Sunday after Epiphany or between 15 and 21 May, Proper 7

Almighty God,
your Son revealed in signs and miracles
the wonder of your saving love.
Renew your people with your heavenly grace,
and in all our weakness
sustain us by your mighty power;
through Jesus Christ our Lord,
who is alive and reigns with you and the Holy Spirit,
one God, now and for ever.

We should take note of the phrase "signs and miracles" as a description of those things which we read of Our Lord in the gospel record. One might wonder why both words are used. Are they there just to give a certain rhythm to the collect? I don't think so. Both words *signs* and *miracles* are important, especially in our age.

In this century, possibly more Christian energy has been spent arguing over the miracles of the gospels than over any other aspect of the faith. All such arguments will forever be futile. We have the gospel record as it has been handed down to us. The incidents which we call miracles have been there from the beginning, and they will be there until the end of time. If we believe that the giving of this gospel record to the people of God was and always will be a supreme gift of God, then we must accept the gift as given. That does not in the least prevent us from valuing some parts of the gift more than others or choosing how we are going to use the gift in various ways, but it does suggest that we allow each other to come to the gospel and draw from it as it speaks to each of us. There is much in the gospel record we will never be able to explain. One of the supreme ironies is that most of our arguing about miracles in the gospel has taken place in a century when the miraculous — in the sense of there being much more then we can explain — has become a commonplace of the age.

I as a late-twentieth-century Christian have been given the miracle stories of the gospels for a reason. There may be many reasons why they are in the record. They may be the description by another culture of certain events which our culture would report differently. They may be the fervent expression of faith of a past generation. They may be many things. But the issue is that if the gospel record is for me the word of God, then there is a reason why I have been given the miracles. The only question, then, on which I should expend thought and energy and prayer is, In what way is this miracle story significant for me in my time? Or, to use the word from this collect, Of what is this miracle a *sign* for me as I read?

Our Lord healed. That is obvious and undeniable. In an age when our capacity to heal is exploding before our eyes and reaching for a new holistic unity, then how are the healings of Jesus to become signs for us? In an age when it is becoming quite obvious that the relationship of our human nature and the created order around us is crucial for the future, then do we spend time wondering whether Our Lord said, ''Peace be still,'' to the storm or to his frightened disciples? We ask instead of what significance, or what sign, that incident can be to a generation facing ecological responsibility. In an age when our capacity to wrestle with death itself is filling us with awe, we do not spend time arguing whether Jesus *really* (a word much beloved by the western mind) raised Lazarus. We take the raising of Lazarus as a sign, as having for us a significance to help us reflect about our own dealings with death and our responses to it.

The real point, expressed beautifully in the collect, is that the gift of the gospel is to ''reveal the wonder of God's saving love . . . to renew God's people . . . and to sustain us . . . through Jesus Christ Our Lord.'' Thanks be to God.

Eighth Sunday after Epiphany or between 22 and 28 May, Proper 8

Almighty God,
grant us the Spirit to think and do always
those things that are right,
that we who can do nothing good without you,
may live according to your holy will;
through Jesus Christ our Lord,
who lives and reigns with you and the Holy Spirit,
one God, now and for ever.

Sometimes the way we Christians express our prayers shows the way in which we think of God's working. As we read the phrase "grant us the Spirit," we can get an idea that God's Holy Spirit is rather elusive, making us pursue, remaining out of sight and giving us tantalizing glimpses, insisting that we do a measure of pleading before coming into our lives.

Nothing could be further from the truth. The Holy Spirit is not a power outside us making us reach for it. The Holy Spirit is within us. We cannot say this too often because this has been a peculiar and stubborn difficulty for western Christians. We tend to think that if we do this or that or the other, if we are very good or very holy or very pious or very prayerful or a score of other vague and worthy things, that the Holy Spirit may possibly deign to come to us. We are wrong. The Holy Spirit is ours by baptism. Once given, the Holy Spirit is ours. We do not retain that Spirit by being whatever we mean by good; nor do we lose the Spirit by being whatever we mean by bad. Granted, we may lose our awareness of possessing the Holy Spirit. We may forget. We may ignore. We may sneer. Not one of these things makes the slightest difference about the Holy Spirit of God dwelling in us or not. When we say, "Grant us the Spirit," we are asking for grace to make use of the Spirit already in us.

"To think and do." Christian faith is always wary of thought by itself, or rather as an end in itself. Thinking is not enough. Gandhi was very fond of talking about *satyagraha*. He said he meant by that the kind of thinking that would not prevent a person from acting on a thought. *Satyagraha* is thought issuing in action. We might recall that the letter which James wrote to the early Christians had a great deal to say about the link between thinking and doing.

"To think and do always those things that are right." Our lives are full of choices as to how we will think and act. Choices are part of the strain of our lives. How often do we take a moment to place a choice before God, even if only in a lightning gesture done wherever we are. We will not always either think or do what is right. We may not know for a long time afterward what would have been "right." We may never know. But if what we decide and do is decided and done with all the integrity and honesty we can muster, then we are right. Rightness before God is something infinitely more than being correct.

"We who can do nothing good without you." At first reading it can almost be heard as an overpassiveness, an acknowledgement of helplessness. It is not meant that way. Whatever good is in you and me is there because of the indwelling of the Holy Spirit.

"May live according to your holy will." Again this can sound an impossible demand. How can I always know God's will in a particular situation? I cannot. What then is being asked of me here as a Christian? When I must make a decision, it is I who must make it. Being a Christian is not some device to get out of human responsibility. The decision must issue from my will. But before it does, I am asked to place the decision before another and greater will — the will of God. By doing that, however quickly and simply, I am invoking the Holy Spirit in my life. I have offered my will to the Spirit's will. When I do that, I am living according to God's holy will. Thanks be to God.

Ninth Sunday after Epiphany or between 29 May and 4 June, Proper 9

> *Lord God of the nations,*
> *you have revealed your will to all people*
> *and promised us your saving help.*
> *May we hear and do what you command,*
> *that the darkness may be overcome*
> *by the power of your light;*
> *through your Son Jesus Christ our Lord,*
> *who lives and reigns with you and the Holy Spirit,*
> *now and for ever.*

"Lord God of the nations." It is a form of address that much modern Christian faith is uneasy with. For many generations God has been thought of in terms of personal piety. God is the source of grace to whom we turn as individuals. One is not questioning that for a moment. God has also been understood as the source and sustainer of creation. Yet in the whole middle zone between creation and personal life, we have not found it easy to think in terms of the presence and action of God. Since most of human life is lived in that middle zone of events and interrelationships and policy making, this has been a significant omission!

Do we believe that the whole area of national and international life is the legitimate domain of God's Holy Spirit? Many things in our society militate against accepting this belief even if we would wish to, the most significant being the marked secularism of our culture. The institutions of religion are marginal to our political discourse and our media. Evidence also suggests that homilizing in Sunday worship on themes other than personal faith — its questions, needs and problems — is minimal. This collect challenges that situation.

"You have revealed your will to all people." This collect pushes us beyond where many Christians feel comfortable. There is no limit placed on those nations of which God is the Lord. If the collect really means all nations, then many of us have some thinking to do, some taking off of small lenses and the donning of larger! We are like the Jews in exile in Babylon, who were forced to put on larger lenses through which to see the universality of God, when Isaiah insisted that Cyrus the Persian was God's instrument to change history. We are also like the early Hebrew Christians, who were forced to see that following the Man of Nazareth was more than continuing as a faithful Jew. Consequently we are forced to look at all contemporary issues in a new way, searching for the will and action of the Holy Spirit within them. Are we prepared to do that?

"May we hear and do what you command." Very effective devices in western culture have helped us to limit a prayer such as this collect to the level of the personal. We have for a long time decreed that "religion" has no place in the political and social areas of life. But if we rephrase that stance to say that *Christian spirituality* has no place in these areas, we realize how meaningless the statement is. By its very nature Christian spirituality includes the fullness of our experience and involvement. There cannot be designated areas of life where Christian spirituality is by some neat mental barrier excluded. If we insist on doing this, then our Christian faith is a neat set of propositions fitted into and subservient to our main and real view of life. If that is the case, then that same main view of life has become a pseudo-spirituality and true Christianity is stifled!

"That the darkness may be overcome by the power of your light." For a Christian the source of light in his or her life is Jesus Christ. Christian vocation is so to live by that light that through our living a portion of that light is released into the world. Our lives may seem tiny in the great scheme of things, but we cannot tell how our faithful word or act may be used by God as a means of grace in circumstances totally beyond our knowing, perhaps not even in our own lifetime. The world is changed toward light or darkness by every single human decision and act. Therefore let us live in the light which is Christ. Thanks be to God.

Ash Wednesday

Almighty and everlasting God,
you despise nothing you have made
and forgive the sins of all who are penitent.
Create and make in us new and contrite hearts,
that we, worthily lamenting our sins
and acknowledging our brokenness,
may obtain of you, the God of all mercy,
perfect remission and forgiveness;
through Jesus Christ our Lord,
who lives and reigns with you and the Holy Spirit,
one God, for ever and ever.

Generosity, acceptance, and affirmation, how very much we welcome these attributes when we find them in another person. Perhaps that is because we are reminded, when we experience these precious and lovely things, that they are attributes of God. In showing them or being shown them, we are reflecting the very nature of God.

These are the attributes of God of which the first three lines of this collect speak. God, for whom we cannot even find adequate language, does not despise our pathetic humanity. In fact God does not despise what we sometimes find it easy to despise. It is salutary to realize this. Every one of us has our secret list of despicable things and people. Every culture has such a list, admitted or not. It can lead to very unpleasant consequences which commence with attitudes of exclusion and rejection and end in places such as the gas ovens of Auschwitz.

God not only does not despise our human limitations but actually affirms us in our humanity, just as a loving parent knows the limitations of his or her children and yet loves and affirms them beyond measure. God, after we have broken our relationship by our human frailty, does not accept us back out of pity or generosity or from any necessity. God longs to do so because of love for us as creatures. There is a mysterious sense in which it is true to say that God is prisoner of that love for us.

This day of ashes has been seen as a time to bemoan the immense gulf between us and God. The ashes are a symbol of that gulf. God is divine essence. We are ashes. All of which is true but must be understood in the surrounding context of God's love. Any gulf is of our making. God has not moved back one step from us. God inhabits the human heart and mind if only as an ignored and unrecognized prisoner. That God has moved from the human situation is a pathetic illusion of our day and culture. The fact that sacred scripture uses the images of the past to speak of God does not mean that God is not present in contemporary reality. The God of the camel caravan in the wilderness of Sinai need not be any less God to me as I journey across the wilderness of the late twentieth century in an economy seat in a Boeing 737. The images have changed, but the eternal properties of God and of our human life have not been diminished by one iota. Holiness, mystery, love, sin, forgiveness are all as much part of contemporary existence as they ever were. They are all about us, mostly in disguise. They surround us, hidden in the language of psychology and sociology, in the pages of countless paperbacks and magazine articles about the human condition.

The second half of the collect shows us to be surrounded by the love of God. Notice how we even turn to God to give us the grace to seek him, so that God can forgive us and bring us back into relationship. We are acknowledging that we need God's grace to seek God's grace! On this opening day of Lent we need to realize not only the obvious and painful fact that we are human and sinful, but also that our humanity and sinfulness exist in the undiminishable love of God. We might do well to dwell on that great truth. God by the very nature of God cannot cease to love us. If we feel ourselves to be spent and useless ashes, then we might remember that those ashes of our humanity lie in the unquenchable fires of God's love. Thanks be to God.

First Sunday in Lent

Almighty God,
whose Son fasted forty days in the wilderness,
and was tempted as we are but did not sin,
give us grace to discipline ourselves
in submission to your Spirit,
that as you know our weakness,
so we may know your power to save;
through Jesus Christ our Lord,
who lives and reigns with you and the Holy Spirit,
one God, now and for ever.

We are with Our Lord in what is always a searching and demanding time of life. He must make choices about the future. He is thirty years of age. John's preaching is calling Jesus out of privacy toward public existence. He is well aware of the opportunities and the dangers of that. He has just submitted himself to the dying and rising experience of baptism in the Jordan. Now he must face the wilderness.

The wilderness surrounded all human existence in the Bible. It lay almost within sight of Jerusalem. For the most part it was desert — hot, rocky, silent, but by no means empty. The desert or the wilderness not only had its own rich, beautiful, and terrible life of insects, animals, and birds; it also had the capacity to invade the inner consciousness of anyone who entered it. Many travelled in it as their home, some entered it as a spiritual way of life. Our Lord dwelt in it to make his choices about the future.

Christian faith says to us that we need to practise self-discipline if we wish to receive something from our wilderness experiences. We do not go to the wilderness always by our own choosing. A sudden marriage crisis, an illness, the loss of a job, and we find ourselves in an emotional, mental, and spiritual wilderness.

"Was tempted as we are." The word *tempted* in the New Testament is very much richer than the word we use today. For us temptation means an invitation and the opportunity to do something wrong. In the New Testament temptation is something far more. It means to be tested in some way. This is the sense in which it is used of Our Lord. During these weeks in the wilderness Jesus has to consider his course of action. He is obviously tested by wrong and unworthy ways to reach his goal. These are what the gospel calls his temptations.

"He did not sin." Again we need to know what is being said here. What are sins in our terms? We human beings make mistakes, know anger and fear, experience alienation from one another and God, feel intense frustration and brokenness. We might say that all these are manifestations of our sinful nature. But they are also true of Jesus. Everyone of these things is a facet of being human. To be sinful, then, cannot mean merely displaying the universal attributes of weakness which emerge from our humanity. We are sinful when we place our will in opposition to the will of God. When self takes command in the face of that which demands we serve other than self, then sin results. When we say that Our Lord did not sin, we are not saying that he lived out an inhuman record of perfection in his responses and emotions and relationships. We are saying that at all times his will was placed under the will of his heavenly Father, unlike each of us whose wills do constant battle with our Father's will. This is exactly why the collect asks for "grace to discipline ourselves in submission to your spirit."

"As you know our weakness so we may know your power." The prayer is subtle and insightful. It says there is one who knows us completely and still accepts and loves us. To know this in our lives, to believe it, to have accepted the fact that we are accepted is immense grace to our impoverished and weak human spirits. This may be the point in our relationship with Our Lord where grace flows to us in its deepest and strongest tide. Thanks be to God.

Second Sunday in Lent

Almighty God,
whose Son was revealed in majesty
before he suffered death upon the cross,
give us faith to perceive his glory,
that being strengthened by his grace
we may be changed into his likeness, from glory to glory;
who lives and reigns with you and the Holy Spirit,
one God, now and for ever.

At the heart of the Christian faith is a world of paradox. It is not for nothing that one of the early words for Christian faith was *mysterion*. Christian faith, although we must try to make it expressible and understandable, is not a set of clearly defined propositions forming attractive handbooks for instruction. While these are and should be written, there is an element which always eludes our best efforts to do that kind of thing.

At the heart of the paradoxes of the gospel is the kingdom of God, the central theme in Our Lord's ministry. Every aspect of that kingdom expresses values which diametrically oppose and subvert the assumptions of our world and time. The first are last; the rich are poor; the sorrowful are joyful. Standing as the utter contradiction of all our assumptions about life is the cross. How can this be?

It is almost impossible for us today to realize how revolting and insulting that symbol of a man on a cross was to men and women of the New Testament world, especially when it was presented to them as a portrait of their Lord and King! Paul knew this, and he wrestles with it many times. But he saw also the power of it as he realized the paradox of it. Its ugliness was beauty, its shame was glory, the prisoner was a king, the cross was a throne.

All concepts of the Messiah — and there were many — agreed at least on a powerful, effective, world-changing figure. Yet here again the early Christians recognized truth behind paradox. The seeming weakness of Jesus was seen to be power, the power to risk oneself and become vulnerable for others. Thus they looked at the cross and perceived a throne. They saw shame but discerned majesty. The collect says that Our Lord was "revealed in majesty before he suffered death."

We now ask for the same gift of spiritual discernment. Sometimes we need it to see through seeming failure in ourselves or in someone else, and to perceive that something has been achieved. As we observe what seems to be someone's crucifixion, perhaps by pain or illness, we may become aware that in a mysterious way we are witnessing a kind of majesty emanating from their person.

It is something of that we are trying to express when we ask for "faith to perceive his glory, that . . . we may be changed into his likeness." We are not asking for the ability to remember some past glory in a past figure. We are praying for the grace to see in contemporary life the elements which made his life glorious. Whatever we saw in him, we ask of our own time and lives where that quality is, where that pattern of response and behaviour is. In other words, we ask where Christ walks now, where he hangs on the cross now, where he rises now in glory. To live with this kind of discernment as a Christian is to perceive the glory of Christ in one's own time and society. It can change one's outlook on life. We begin to look at things from a Christian perspective. We learn in some small way to see things through Our Lord's eyes. If this be true, then we may think of ourselves as being "changed into his likeness from glory to glory," even if only in the sense that we begin to detect, beyond our common reality, a great and more mysterious reality which we call glory. Thanks be to God.

Third Sunday in Lent — Year A

Almighty God,
whose Son Jesus Christ gives the water of eternal life,
may we always thirst for you,
the spring of life and source of goodness;
through him who lives and reigns with you
and the Holy Spirit,
one God, now and for ever.

All through these Lenten collects we are being addressed in a way which our culture and time does not find particularly easy to grasp. It is a way with which many people who are fine and good and deeply spiritual still have difficulty. It is the way of symbols. Many of us are happier when we are addressed in a more straightforward way. We like information. Symbols themselves are a kind of information. It is just that they inform in a different way. This collect begins by saying that Our Lord Jesus "gives the water of eternal life." What does that mean?

As we begin to answer the question, we immediately realize that symbols and images involve us. We have to bring ourselves to them and perhaps do a little wrestling with them. Information can remain outside us. We receive and either accept or reject it, but we do not need to become involved with it. However, as soon as we are engaged by a great universal symbol such as water, we are drawn into it, if only because we are immediately searching for the meaning which water has in our own experience.

As we try to grasp what it may mean to say that Our Lord gives us water, we begin to recall episodes in our lives involving water. Water enclosed us in the womb. From those waters we came to our present life. Ever since then water has been life for us. It has washed our bodies, refreshed us, slaked our thirst, cooled us. Water has carried us on its surface, supported us as we swam. In seas and oceans water has moved us with its beauty, spoken to us in its peace, and awed us by its storms.

All such images of water have to do with our ongoing temporal lives. We then take all these images of water and try to see them in terms of our relationship with Our Lord. Hymns do this a great deal. Read the hymn "Fairest Lord Jesus" as an example.

So I ask all the images of water in my life how they speak of Our Lord. I have been born as a Christian in the womb of Christ. Ever since then my spirit has been fed by his grace. I have needed his purity to wash me. I have needed his strength to restore my flagging faith. I have needed his truth to satisfy my thirst for a renewed faith or a sense of meaning. Christ has often supported me, held me up like water. There are times when my Lord, as the sea or the ocean, has moved me with his beauty, spoken to me by his peace or *shalom*, and awed me with his power and majesty.

The next part of the collect remains in symbolic language. When we say, "May we always thirst for you," we are saying far more than, "May we always go on gathering more and more information about you." When we pray that Christ may be for us the "spring of life," what does it mean for each one of us? That phrase immediately transports me to a cool shady hollow where I went every day during the summer months for drinking water for the farmhouse. There — cool, deep, still, and silent — was the well into which I dipped the white, carefully washed bucket. The clear water rushed in and filled the bucket to overflowing, taxing my childhood arms to haul it up the bank. That for me will be a lifelong image of Christ being the "spring of life," the source of grace for me. What does the phrase bring to your mind? If there comes a moment in your experience which gives meaning to those words, then you will have grasped the idea of Our Lord as spring and source far more effectively than if it were explained and analysed for you. Thanks be to God.

Third Sunday in Lent — Years B and C

Father of mercy,
alone we have no power in ourselves to help ourselves.
When we are discouraged by our weakness,
strengthen us to follow Christ,
our pattern and our hope;
who lives and reigns with you and the Holy Spirit,
one God, now and for ever.

The mood of the collect is in keeping with the fact that we are at the midpoint of a very sombre season. Not sad but certainly sombre, because we are dealing with the most serious things in our human experience.

Somehow Lent is actually the pattern of our life's pilgrimage, a road which we take consciously at this time of year. We follow the human steps of Our Lord as he wrestles with his own humanity. We go with him into wilderness where both he and we must try to find the right path if we are to respond to the will of God for us. We sit with him by the well of Sychar, sharing his thirst as well as his concern that an able but confused woman understand herself and the will of God for her life. So far these have been two stopping places on our journey with Our Lord. Wherever we pause in this Lenten pilgrimage, there is always before us our final stopping place. Down the highway of Lent there looms a hill, and on that hill are three crosses. Those crosses wait for us to approach as they waited for Our Lord. This mutual knowledge of the waiting crosses joins his and our humanity. The cross is the tragic element at the heart of Our Lord's life and of ours. He and we must suffer.

There are then some reasons for the sombre note of Lent and this collect. We are brought to the realization of our humanity even as we are brought to realizing his. We begin by saying something about ourselves that in our most thoughtful moments terrifies us. We acknowledge that in some sense we are alone.

To be human is to know aloneness. Perhaps most sombrely we hear Wilde's voice saying, "Nothing begins and nothing ends that is not paid with moan, for we are born in another's pain and we perish in our own." As a description of human experience that is not necessarily wrong but it is very inadequate. It does, however, emphasise the fact of aloneness which can often cloud our lives.

All this is to speak of our capacity for aloneness as human beings, even when we are among many others. There is another aloneness, that of assuming that there is no source of grace outside ourselves or outside the human situation. Today we would probably call this existential aloneness. It is that state which we describe by saying that we are "without God in the world." Making that assumption the collect tells us with brutal directness that "we have no power in ourselves to help ourselves." Alone, in that deeply spiritual sense of being without God, we are powerless.

We cannot help sometimes encountering the feeling of the absence of God. God is never absent but our sense of God's presence can falter, sometimes even shatter entirely. Usually the cause is discernible, but sometimes there is no definable reason that we can discover. Suddenly we are alone in a desert. It can be agony. Such extreme experiences are rare in our lives. Usually such times can better be defined as when "we are discouraged by our weakness."

Christian faith is not a facile way to avoid such times. We cannot get away from ourselves, but we can invite Our Lord to come to us. In the language of the collect we can use Our Lord's life to give us a different pattern of handling our situation. To do that is first of all to end the alone-ness. That in itself may actually begin to change our pattern of behaviour. That could well be the first step of our climb out of the spiritual pit we find ourselves in. Thanks be to God.

Fourth Sunday in Lent — Year A

Almighty God,
through the waters of baptism
your Son has made us children of light.
May we ever walk in his light
and show forth your glory in the world;
through Jesus Christ our Lord,
who is alive and reigns with you and the Holy Spirit,
one God, now and for ever.

Christian liturgy attempts to express great truths which are both mysteries and universals. Usually liturgy touches something at the heart of all human experience. It may be the mystery of love, forgiveness, death, resurrection. The deepest mystery in the faith is the person and work of Our Lord Jesus Christ.

"Through the waters of baptism your Son has made us children of light." Jesus gave us only three specific commands. He commanded us to eat and drink the bread and wine of Eucharist, to love one another, and to baptize. He himself went through the strange, ancient, and beautiful ritual whereby our birth from the waters of the womb is re-enacted. Baptism began a new chapter in his life. In a sense he came from the waters of the Jordan a new man. We believe that when we offer ourselves for Christian baptism, we wish to make a great change in our lives. We wish to change direction, to be renewed. Above all we wish to identify our lives with the living reality which Jesus Christ has become for us. In him we have found a guiding light, a light of inspiration, and we wish to embody that same light. Such might be an attempt to spell out the meaning of the first statement in this collect.

It is important to point out the significance of the words "your Son has made us." What is being said here is frequently not understood in Christian experience. It is a mysterious and beautiful truth summed up in Our Lord's own saying to his disciples, "You have not chosen me. I have chosen you." When we offer ourselves for baptism or even for the renewing of our baptismal vows taken in childhood, it is not that we have chosen Our Lord and that he responds by giving us grace. Christian faith believes that even the initial decision we make to seek Our Lord is the work of the Holy Spirit within us, sowing the seed and encouraging us toward Our Lord.

"May we ever walk in his light." There are two words which describe the process of Christian faith. They are inseparable if we are to live out that faith. The words are *conversion* and *sanctification*. Conversion is the name of the time of our decision, when we decide to commit ourselves to Christ as Lord. Sanctification is the living out of that decision in the following years, ideally to our life's ending. But there can also be a time of living before conversion. In many lives the moment of decision has been made possible by a long period of reflection and maturing. Both conversion and sanctification are often a process rather than a single event.

In an age when many are searching for faith and may consider baptism, it is essential that baptism be understood as an event framed in a life-long process or journey. To express the image which is used in the collect — we are a people who spend time looking for a light because we have a sense of lostness or shadow in our lives. We find that light in the person of Jesus Christ. We decide that we wish to walk in that light, and we begin to do so. For what purpose? The collect replies, "To show forth your glory in the world." Christian baptism and Christ's grace are not a sacred therapy to enhance our self-development. They are for the glorifying of Our Lord through our response to him lived out in our daily lives. That a great deal accrues to us spiritually through the living out of such a life is tribute to the overflowing generosity of Our Lord and his Holy Spirit. Thanks be to God.

Fourth Sunday in Lent — Years B and C

Gracious Father,
whose blessed Son Jesus Christ came from heaven
to be the true bread which gives life to the world,
evermore give us this bread,
that he may live in us, and we in him,
who lives and reigns with you and the Holy Spirit,
one God, now and for ever.

This collect is formed by taking a moment of conversation between Jesus and his disciples in an episode given to us in the Gospel according to John.

The conversation is a good example of something being said on one level and being heard on another. A symbolic reference made by Our Lord is interpreted by his disciples only on the factual level, and Our Lord has to help them find his meaning. John is fond of such moments. He tells us of Our Lord once offering the living water of spiritual grace in his conversation with the woman at the well near Sychar. She does not understand. She responds as if he were talking about water in the actual well. Likewise in this episode Jesus is chatting with his disciples about the significance of bread. They recall how God supplied a kind of bread to their ancestors in the form of manna. Jesus says that there is another kind of bread that they can have if they wish. They miss the point at first, until Jesus tells them that he is referring to the spiritual nourishment he can give them. He speaks of "true bread" available to them.

"True bread . . . from heaven." What does this conversation of Our Lord and his disciples mean for us who say this collect? What are we praying for? Obviously we are seeking that grace which comes from a relationship with Our Lord. But what does it mean to be offered the bread of Christ? We know that it cannot mean only literal bread, although we realize that it most certainly includes that. The availability of bread, if we mean the just allocation of resources in our society, is a paramount Christian issue.

"Evermore give us this bread." Christian faith, then, is a spiritual bread. As we say this, we might remember the instructions given to Israel for the gathering of manna. They could gather enough for only one day at a time. If they tried to hoard the manna, it would rot. So much spirituality teaches us of the "dailyness" of life — doing daily exercise for our bodies, having a daily quiet time, setting out to encounter Our Lord daily in some aspect of our experience no matter how simple or ordinary.

"True bread which gives life to the world." The lifestyles we choose can either nourish and grace the world or contribute to its impoverishment. Perhaps the current expression, "being a consumer," is exactly the opposite of what this collect means by "being bread."

"Jesus Christ . . . true bread." Nowhere are bread and the person of Christ linked more than in the Eucharist. One wonders if Jesus thought about this conversation when he and his disciples were together on the last night of his life, and when he decided to link himself to them and to us forever by the symbol of bread.

"That he may live in us, and we in him." This is what he was preparing for that night. He who had lived among us would now live within us. But his life in us would not be a dependent life. It is not as if we give Our Lord life by accepting and following him. Even our accepting him is a sign of his eternal life in us — nourishing, leading, attracting, renewing. Christ does not live by us. He lives in us so that we are enabled to live by him. Thanks be to God.

Fifth Sunday in Lent — Year A

Almighty God,
your Son came into the world
to free us all from sin and death.
Breathe upon us with the power of your Spirit,
that we may be raised to new life in Christ,
and serve you in holiness and righteousness all our days;
through the same Jesus Christ, our Lord.

Sometimes we will have just read something and will be arrested by it. We will realize that we have come across an item of immense significance and have very nearly made the mistake of taking it totally for granted.

"Almighty God, your Son came into the world." We have just stated the mystery of the Incarnation. It is the furnace, the power source of Christian faith. Take that away, and while Christian faith will not disappear, it will of necessity become something else. Notice the simplicity of the language in this opening statement of the collect. Perhaps the greater the truth, the greater the simplicity needed. Here we see six short words hold the shining truth of Christian faith. The words are of a piece with the simplicity of the event itself, the manger and stable, the man and woman by whose love the child is nourished. But the very simplicity serves to let the wonder shine out for those who are prepared to linger, to look through the simple event to the infinite and mysterious meaning.

It is important at this stage on our Lenten journey to take time to realize again the identity of the companion with whom we travel. Soon we will go through the darkest passage of this journey. We will stand by as he is crucified. We will watch others as their world disintegrates. We will

then share extraordinary encounters with them. We, as
they, will become aware of the presence of one whom we
and they thought dead. We and they will kneel and touch
and fear and wonder. All this will take place within days
from the time when we say this collect. It is important to
be aware of who our companion is. This is Jesus our friend,
and at the same time it is Christ the Lord. In this person
God and our humanity are in such harmony that each flows
fully into the other as they meet in front of us in human
flesh.

"To free us all from sin and death." To free us all? I
live twenty centuries after the event spoken of in this collect. How am I to be freed by this event? What has his life
got to do with mine in the sense of affecting it?

It is paramount for us to realize that the eternal mystery we know as the second person of the Holy Trinity did
not become merely a man. In Jesus of Nazareth the divine
mystery assumed our humanity. That is a very different
statement. A mere man would be locked into a particular
history. Jesus lived in a particular history; there is no denying that. But when God became man in such a history and
such a place, God through that man entered into humanity. Jesus is not merely a person in whom God dwells. Jesus
is the gateway through which God enters by means of a
particular human life into all of human life.

What Jesus was, therefore, has entered into humanity
forever. We might reach for an analogy. A healing antibi-
otic has to enter my body at one point, but then it travels
through all of my body seeking out the places where it must
do battle with that which threatens me. Such is my Lord.
The Lord is divine, eternal, grace-giving, health-bringing
medicine flowing in the total stream of humanity, through
all human affairs and all human history. It meets me in my
particular humanity and in my particular circumstances, and
it is more than capable of bringing healing to me in the
shadows and the dark infections of my single and particular life. Thanks be to God.

Fifth Sunday in Lent — Years B and C

> *Most merciful God,*
> *by the death and resurrection*
> *of your Son Jesus Christ,*
> *you created humanity anew.*
> *May the power of his victorious cross*
> *transform those who turn in faith*
> *to him who lives and reigns with you*
> *and the Holy Spirit,*
> *one God, now and for ever.*

In the medieval world, images meant a great deal. Since most people in those centuries could not read, much Christian communication was expressed in images. Among the greatest and most used of these images, if not the greatest, was the cross of Christ. To display the cross was in itself a significant act. Response was demanded, whether of adoration as a believer or attack as an enemy. The cross did not allow one to ignore it. The reason for this was that the cross was regarded very much as we today would regard any immensely powerful world-changing force, such perhaps as a nuclear reactor. That may at first hearing seem a very strange analogy, but if one thinks about it again, it may sound less strange. Each is seen as something tremendously significant. Each is capable of transforming human society and human history, albeit in very different ways and by very different strengths. Each is more powerful than those who would tame and use it for their own ends. Each speaks terrifyingly of both death and life. Each shows both the dark and the glorious sides of human nature.

Nowadays in the sequence of the Christian year, we speak very seldom of the cross and passion of Our Lord. Good Friday is naturally such a time, and Holy Cross Day also. But the collect for today calls us to consider this again.

The heart of the Christian faith is centred around the events of Our Lord's life and death and resurrection. The place of his death is the cross. It is absolutely essential that anyone claiming to be Christian knows the meaning of what took place on that cross. By itself the cross as the centre of Christian attention is incomplete. The total image must be that of the cross and the garden tomb. One is the terrible gateway to death, the other the glorious portal from death to risen life. That is why, even though this collect is still separated from Easter by the whole process of Our Lord's passion, it nevertheless has us speak in one breath of the "death and resurrection of your Son Jesus Christ."

What does this event mean for a Christian? The collect responds simply and succinctly, yet it captures the majesty of the achievement. By the events of the crucifixion and the resurrection, Our Lord "created humanity anew." Language can hide immensity unless we linger and reflect on the words. Think of the extraordinary reality these words are trying to convey, nothing less than the remaking of humanity. How is such a thing possible?

One might begin by forming an image of humanity which ironically is once again comprehensible to modern people to a far greater extent than at any time over the last few centuries. If it is possible to say in a few words what the single great new realization of our culture might be, it is our seeing more and more clearly that all creation is a vast interconnected web, an ecosystem. Think then of humanity itself as a web, not merely millions of separate individuals but a vast web. Then extend that web back and forward in time to past and future generations. We have now imaged a concept of humanity as an entity, a totality. Whatever happens at any point on the web affects the whole web. Christian faith says that the whole web has been affected by two events. We call them our fall or failure and our redemption or salvation. In the infancy of our humanity we, under the names Adam and Eve, damaged the bridge between us and God. We did not break it; we damaged it. For a Christian, Christ is the one through whom God fixed the bridge. That image by no means explains the wonder of all this. It is merely an attempt to forge a helpful tool to begin to grasp it. What is important is that the damaged relationship is renewed. Humanity is renewed. Thanks be to God.

The Sunday of the Passion
With the Liturgy of the Palms

Almighty and everliving God,
in tender love for all our human race
you sent your Son our Saviour Jesus Christ
to take our flesh
and suffer death upon a cruel cross.
May we follow the example of his great humility,
and share in the glory of his resurrection;
through Jesus Christ our Lord,
who is alive and reigns with you and the Holy Spirit,
one God, now and for ever.

If we look at the language of this collect, perhaps reading it three or four times in rapid succession, we discover something. It moves all the time. Every image in it is one of process, progression, journey. Perhaps this is not wholly accidental because the collect is being said within the movement of a procession on this Sunday.

Liturgical processions are not just occasional attempts to vary the sequence of our liturgy. A procession is full of symbolism in action. It may not be a very grand procession. There may be a small choir, a few children, a server in the latest runners under an ill-fitting alb or cassock, all followed by a very ordinary and very familiar priest. Grandeur and appearance are not the point. Meaning lies in the actual doing of the procession. The very important fact being acted out is that Christian life is a *journey*. We are travellers, "companions on the journey," as a modern hymn sings. The way in which we are doing our travelling may change. At times we may travel as wanderers, rather lost and vulnerable. We may travel as pilgrims, sure of our destination. We may travel as nomads, barely surviving as we go. Sometimes we may be confident enough to travel as adventurers, even explorers. All these modes are true of our Christian travelling. All are implicit in that ordinary shambling procession on its way up the aisle, across by the front pew, back around the font, and finally into the chancel and home!

Consider now the majestic procession in the first line of this collect. We say of Our Lord that he was "crucified yet entered into glory." It may help to realize what crucifixion meant in that long-ago culture. It was looked on rather as some would look today on one dying of AIDS in our culture. It meant one suffered utter rejection and utter shame. As an entry point to glory of any conceivable kind, one could not imagine anything less likely. To be publicly crucified was to be placed utterly outside human respect.

Yet this is the entry through which Our Lord chose to go. He did choose it. It is important to remember that. He walked toward that terrible entry point of the cross. He almost embraced it freely. That is not to say that he did not suffer the terrible fear and pain we would feel. Yet he goes toward the entry point, and when he returns from the unknown realm beyond that terrible door, it is obvious that he has progressed to another state of being.

"May we, walking in the way of the cross, find it is for us the way of life." We have considered Our Lord's progression or journey. Now we consider our own. Christian faith is immediately presented to us as an action, a walking, a progression, a journeying. It is not just any journeying. It is a journey that tries to reflect the terms of his journey. We do not walk any way, we walk in his way, which we believe to be "the way of life." Put even more simply, if we want to live the way we were created to live and are meant to live, then for us this way, his way, is the way.

It is a costly way. It is "the way of the cross." It is neither easy nor attractive, nor is it popular. There are many who would not even consider it a very intelligent way. But it is there in front of us until the end of time, because he first went this way. Before us are his footsteps. We make our own choice of journey. All we know for certain is that many who have tried his way have found it to be "the way of life."

The Great Vigil of Easter

Eternal Giver of life and light,
this holy night shines with the radiance of the risen Christ.
Renew your Church with the Spirit given to us in baptism,
that we may worship you in sincerity and truth,
and shine as a light in the world;
through Jesus Christ our Lord,
who is alive and reigns with you and the Holy Spirit,
one God, now and for ever.

If ever a collect needed to be sung rather than said, it is this one. The language is lyrical, the images are alive and, to use a word within the collect itself, absolutely *radiant*.

"Eternal giver of life and light." All ascriptions at the beginning of prayers draw a quick vivid portrait of God. To say "eternal giver" of God is to pay tribute to the generosity of God, an overflowing generosity, an inability to do other than give. To say that God is "the eternal giver of life" is to show God as the source from which creativity pours without ceasing. Recently I saw an underwater shot of one of the fissures between the tectonic plates of the planet. Deep under the oceans, there are points at which heat flows out of the fires deep within the earth. All around the fissure there is warm water pouring up into the ocean, and in this area life of every conceivable kind abounds. That is the image this line brings to me.

To say that God is "the eternal giver of light" is to portray God in the most ancient of ways. None of us needs to be told of the power of light to transform everything including our moods, our ability to function, our hold on life, our relationships with others. No wonder the ancients thought of light as itself a god. The Bible does not lessen our attitude toward light. Light is one of the great realities specifically made by God in the story of creation. The Bible, however, directs us back beyond the light to worship the creator of the light.

"This holy night shines with the radiance of the risen Christ." Even the words *holy night* are an echo of another night when light shone — the occasion of the mystery we call incarnation. That was the night of the first birth, the first blazing of this light. This night is the second birth, the new birth, the second blazing of the light which is Jesus Christ. Indeed, if we include his transfiguration, it is the third blazing of this light. There can be more echoes for us from that other holy night in Bethlehem. On that night he lay in a manger, on this night in a tomb. On that night he was wrapped in the swaddling clothes of a child, on this night in the linens of the dead. From both manger and tomb he grows, rises, and shines in the world. Both swaddling clothes and grave clothes are shed, and instead he is clothed in royal robes, in light, and in majesty. On that long ago night shepherds and wise men came. On this night of resurrection millions come. Again and again these two nights echo one another.

"Renew your church with the Spirit given to us in baptism." In what sense is the church able to become the place of his contemporary rising. The fact that this question is asked reminds us that the church is quite capable of becoming Our Lord's tomb, the place where the memory of him lies buried behind great stones of many kinds of deadness. Can we be reminded again in a living and exciting way of our baptism, of what it calls us to, of its lifelong demand on us, of its being far more than a mere memory? Can we be brought to realize what our baptism unrelentingly demands of us? There are two things the collect mentions. It demands first of all that we worship not through a deadly sense of bored stubborn duty, but by giving ourselves wholeheartedly — meaning it, enjoying it, celebrating in more than just a formal official sense. The second thing is that the same worship may send us out into the other six days knowing that we can, if we choose, be light rather than darkness in the world. This collect is in fact talking about nothing less than your resurrection and mine — now, today. Thanks be to God.

Second Sunday of Easter

Almighty and eternal God,
the strength of those who believe
and the hope of those who doubt,
may we, who have not seen, have faith
and receive the fullness of Christ's blessing,
who is alive and reigns with you and the Holy Spirit,
one God, now and for ever.

One of the great and compassionate marks of holy scripture is its realism about human nature. There is no pretending in the Bible. There are no impossible standards of human perfection which communicate frustration and resentment even before one begins to try to reach them. All the great heroic figures of the Bible have one thing in common. Their weaknesses as well as their strengths are shown to us with sometimes brutal clarity. One of the realities of our human condition which the Bible readily reveals is doubt. Notice the wonderfully wise balance in the opening statement of this collect. It refers to God as "the strength of those who believe and the hope of those who doubt."

Faith and doubt are very close companions. As a matter of fact, one cannot exist without the other. Faith, if it is really faith, exists in the constant presence of doubt. Faith could not continue if there were no doubt. We realize that to doubt is not something monstrous to be hidden. Doubt is natural and normal. There is a kind of faith which is so near to doubt that it will do anything to hide and deny this! Often a faith that is very belligerently expressed, that claims utter sureness and utter security, that denies the validity of anything that differs from its own stance is highly likely to be a precarious faith. It shouts loud to dispel the frightening voices of doubt within itself. A mature faith, one that knows doubt to be the companion which sometimes visits faith, is ready to accept such company from time to time, knowing that faith will return if it is sought. We most often think of faith and doubt as existing in different people. Actually we would be wiser and much nearer the truth if we acknowledged that all of us play both roles from time to time. "Faith," Peter Abelard used to say in his University of Paris lectures, "is a house we come to as we journey through the forest of doubt."

"May we who have not seen, have faith." We often wish that we could have been there, that we could have held the baby, listened to the teacher, sat at that table, rowed in those lake boats, even stood near that cross, terrible as it was. Most of all we wish we could have been in that room where he appeared. Suppose we could actually have touched him. Suppose we could have sat on the beach at the lake and shared that breakfast in the dawn. If we could only have done that, would not Christian faith be easy. Would it? Was it easy for them, easy for Peter later on, easy for Paul? Was it easy even for Thomas in later years? Of course not. Because faith is not just knowing something as information. Faith is living out what you know, and that is sometimes far from easy.

But maybe we should stay a while thinking about them, the men and women who did share breakfast, who did sit at the table with him, who did chat, who did gaze in awe at him in front of those locked doors. Those men and women are supremely important to us because theirs was the faith which ignited succeeding faith. And what do they say to us? They say a resounding yes to faith, yes to his being alive among them, yes to his being their Lord. Their yes has ignited other affirmatives in every generation. One of those who said their own yes came in contact with our lives at some stage, and we too, perhaps all unknowingly, said our yes to Christ as Lord. When that happens we are not digging into the remote past for proofs about him. We don't need to do that. We have encountered him. We know him. The Bible does not have Job say, ''I know that my Redeemer lived.'' Job, and we, can say, ''I know that my Redeemer lives.'' Thanks be to God.

Third Sunday of Easter

O God,
your Son made himself known to his disciples
in the breaking of bread.
Open the eyes of our faith,
that we may see him in his redeeming work,
who is alive and reigns with you and the Holy Spirit,
one God, now and for ever.

There is an old hymn which begins in a way that sounds quaint to us, but it has great beauty and teaches a great truth. It begins "Lord, when thou didst thyself undress." The reference, of course, is to the Incarnation, that mysterious event when, as we believe, God took off the garments of godhead and chose the garment, or the body, of humanity.

Clothes are important to us all. We dress as presentably as we can. We do not like to be caught out in clothes unsuitable to the way we wish to appear at a given time. We know that a great deal is communicated by the way we dress.

God undressed. What does that mean? First that undressing could not have been otherwise than an exchanging of unimaginably fine clothing for pathetic coverings. Such is the gulf between the shining of divinity and the dulness of humanity. But why do it? Because God wished to "make himself known" to us. People dressed as we are make us feel comfortable. We are easy in their company. They communicate to us and we to them. In such simple terms can we begin to understand the unimaginable gift of incarnation.

"Your Son made himself known to his disciples." He

did indeed, totally. He kept nothing back, hid nothing, even the weakness and vulnerability that his choosing of human-ity involved. All of him was shared with us. He showed us his exhaustion, his anger, his disappointments, his depression, his fear. He showed us himself naked and dying, devoid of dignity and majesty. He showed us his dead body.

But he let us see other things too. He showed his intimacy with the Father. He showed his power to heal. In the episode we call transfiguration, he revealed the inner majesty hidden away beneath the humanity. He showed iron self-discipline and calm under intense pressure. He showed immense courage and resolution. Our Lord most certainly made himself known to his disciples.

But the collect takes one moment above all others. He made himself known "in the breaking of bread." Every-thing else about the evening was familiar. The meal itself, the occasion, the things said, the little traditional actions done — all were familiar to them and had been since child-hood. But suddenly there came something that was not familiar. He was on his feet. He was quietly saying some-thing so terrible that, like us to this day, they probably never fully understood. He said that he himself was the meal. He was the food and drink, the bread and wine. Bread broken now, himself broken tomorrow. Wine poured now, his blood poured tomorrow. This is the ultimate moment of making himself known.

One of the marks of our worship today is our repeated return to this moment. We have become again a eucharis-tic church, centred on this mystery that is so simple and yet so profound. Perhaps there is a taste of irony in the fact that we dress a little more elaborately for its celebration. We even talk of dressing the altar. Yet in this celebration we are showing forth what that old hymn presented to us as "the undressing of Our Lord." The king takes off his royal robes and dons our so much lesser garments, doing it for one reason, out of his great love for us, and with the determination to reach out to us in the only way that we in our limitations and in our poverty could receive. Thanks be to God.

Fourth Sunday of Easter

O God of peace,
who brought again from the dead our Lord Jesus Christ,
that great shepherd of the sheep,
by the blood of the eternal covenant,
make us perfect in every good work to do your will,
and work in us that which is well-pleasing in your sight;
through Jesus Christ our Lord.

These collects after Easter tend to show how the resurrection of Our Lord gives us certain gifts. Beginning with the collect for Easter Day we realize the gift is (1) a new freedom from the grip of sin and death. Then in the succeeding weeks the resurrection gifts are (2) resources to struggle with doubt, (3) the Eucharist itself, and now this week, (4) the concept of Our Lord as shepherd in terms of caring, nurture, love.

"O God of peace." We might have expected such a collect to begin with the words, "O God of power." After all, the resurrection of Our Lord is an act of immense power. Why then the rather unexpected ascription, "O God of peace." To respond we have first to remind ourselves that the English word *peace* and the Hebrew word *shalom* are somewhat different. *Peace*, as we use the word, is only a small part of *shalom*. To say that God is the God of *shalom* is to suggest that God brings all things into unity and harmony. God gives things their ultimate meaning and pattern. When we say that this same God is the God who brought from the dead Our Lord Jesus Christ, we understand that in doing so God, as it were, healed a certain wound in the universe. God repaired a brokenness in creation. God made things one again, or brought things into harmony again.

What things? What was brought into harmony or repaired or healed? Christian faith answers that the relationship between humanity and God was healed. Our Lord took upon himself our human nature, took it through the years of a human life, met death with it, and then showed that our human nature, lived in the way he had lived it, was capable of moving through death to something greater, something from which he was able to return. Our Lord showed us that human life, if it be lived in complete commitment to the will of God rather than the will of the self, becomes something else, something that in an extraordinary way is no longer under the thrall of sin and death. Can we ever explain that? I think not, but that is the central mystery of what we call the Incarnation.

The collect then tells us two things about the resurrection of Our Lord. First, that in doing this for us, in accepting human life, living it out on our terms, facing even death with it, returning to us from that death, Our Lord shows his caring for our humanity to be beyond words. He is our shepherd. As John said to us, ''Greater love has no man than this, that a man lay down his life for his friends.''

The second thing the collect tells us is the great cost of the resurrection. Without Jesus' death there could be no resurrection. Without the cross there could be no opening tomb. The cost of all the gifts of the resurrection given to us is Our Lord's blood. That is the simple and terrible ''bottom line,'' as we would say, of Christian faith. Nowadays we are apt to be somewhat patronizing toward those images once used very freely about Our Lord's sacrifice. We tend to shy away from the old hymn, ''There is a fountain filled with blood,'' or at the banner which proclaims ''blood and fire,'' or at statements such as ''the blood of Christ cleanses us from all sins.'' But when we have had our intellectual smile, the truth remains that we are Christian today because the blood of Jesus Christ was actually spilled to make our Christian faith possible. Thanks be to God.

Fifth Sunday of Easter

Almighty God,
your Son Jesus Christ is the way, the truth, and the life.
Give us grace to love one another
and walk in the way of his commandments,
who lives and reigns with you and the Holy Spirit,
one God, now and for ever.

There is always something vivid and immediate about dialogue. It brings people much nearer to us than mere narrative. This collect emerges out of a conversation. Our Lord has been speaking with the disciples about himself. He mentions the way that he must go, and suddenly Philip bursts out in exasperation that they simply do not know what that way is. Our Lord turns to him and says the words which form the opening statement of this collect.

"I am the way, the truth, and the life." It is one of those tightly packed statements of Our Lord, like "this is my body" and "the kingdom of God is within you." The sentences sound so simple, but when we reflect on them, they are like great deep wells of meaning.

"I am the way." We who have inherited nearly twenty centuries of Christianity can hardly imagine the first years of the movement. Try to think of a Christianity without visible churches, without seminaries, prayer books, hymn books, without endless books of theological reflection. Try to imagine a very much simpler situation, where the followers of the Nazarene try to decide without any precedents what they should do, how they should behave, what Our Lord wishes them to be, how they should respond to a thousand unanswered questions of thought and behaviour. They live as a tiny minority in the great cities of the Roman

Empire, gathering to share the bread and wine and to tell the stories of their Lord. In a word, what are they seeking? They are seeking for a way to be Christian. Because people watching them realized this, these early followers of Our Lord became known as The Way. People saw that these men and women had somehow found a way to live life with joy and meaning in a world where both were in short supply! What are the chances of people calling Christians The Way in the late twentieth century? The most likely societies for that to happen in are those where there is once again some cost to being Christian.

Does the phrase "the way" speak to our personal situation as Christians? Does believing in Jesus Christ as Lord entail a certain way of life? Does it mean a certain way of dealing with our possessions, handling our relationships, carrying out our professional lives? In what ways does being Christian affect my thinking, my decisions, my behaviour? Simple straightforward questions, even rather obvious, you might feel, but reasonable and necessary from time to time.

"I am the truth." All our lives are a search for the truth, the truth about ourselves, about life, about our relationships, about what we should aim for in life? Every now and again we come across somebody or something that our inner self says is true, in the sense of possessing integrity and reality. For a Christian Our Lord is the ultimate embodiment of that kind of truth. He is ultimately all that the best of me searches for and wants to be.

"I am the life." Everything in our lives has a source. We say of some trait, some aspect of our personality, that it comes from such and such a source — another family member, a book we read, a teacher we had, and so on. For a Christian, Our Lord is the source of the most essential and valued aspects of his or her life. Our Lord is the life from which a Christian draws life at its deepest level. For Our Lord is the way, the truth, and the life. Thanks be to God.

Sixth Sunday of Easter

Merciful God,
you have prepared for those who love you
riches beyond imagination.
Pour into our hearts such love toward you,
that we, loving you above all things,
may obtain your promises,
which exceed all that we can desire;
through Jesus Christ our Lord,
who is alive and reigns with you and the Holy Spirit,
one God, now and for ever.

Love is one of life's great mysteries, perhaps *the* mystery. Loving others we can understand. We know that when love is present it transforms life and relationships. The consequences of its absence we know all too well. But loving God? What does it mean to love God? That is not an easy question to answer. Loving God will mean far more than merely believing God exists. What could this "far more" be? It could mean deciding to live one's life on the assumption that God exists, that God is creator, that God has a purpose for creation, and that within creation God has a purpose for one's own life. To live in that way means that one is betting one's life on God. Loving God could also mean constantly giving God glory for what we see in creation or in the lives of others. Loving God could mean setting aside time to enter into a conscious encounter with the presence of God.

The catechism in the *Book of Common Prayer* used to say that one's duty toward God "is to believe in God, to fear God, and to love God with all my heart, mind, soul, and strength; to worship God, to give God thanks, to put my whole trust in God, to call upon God, to honour God's holy name and word, and to serve God truly all the days of my life.'' That is still as fine and complete an answer as can be given to someone who wants to know how to love God.

The collect says that the person who loves God in this way will receive certain riches. If this is not to remain merely pleasant religious language, we must try to define those riches. What is meant here? The primary gift of a love for God is a deep sense of meaning and purpose in a person's life. Within that life there are such invaluable possessions as trust and faith — both generally in short supply in a time of much mistrust and despair. Within that life will be such activities as worship and prayer. The supreme gift of these two activities is that they direct us away from ourselves, beyond our clamouring ego and its demands and needs. The centre of existence moves from being merely within ourselves. We can never escape from a sense of existence as being deeply rooted in ourselves. To ask that this change is asking for the impossible, although there are rare souls who seem to have almost totally escaped from self and self-will. For most of us, our attempts to love God will at least shift our centre of existence from being anchored solely in the self to being anchored in both the self and the higher will of God. We will constantly be drawn between the two, but we will at least have spiritual resources to battle the insatiable demands of the self.

In effect, the collect gives us a kind of equation. The degree to which we love God is the degree to which God can enable us and enrich us spiritually. We are not being told that as much as we can bring ourselves to love God, so much can God love us. God's love for us is without limit and longs to offer itself to us. If we could ''love God above all things,'' then we would ''obtain promises which exceed all that we can desire.'' Somewhere between where we are and that ultimate relationship, most of us live out our groping Christian lives, battling the demands of self-will, sometimes winning a small victory and tasting for a moment the joy of the presence of God. To say this is not in the least to dismiss Christian experience as something pathetic and spasmodic. It is a description of reality. Our journey is toward the city of God, but we are given only glimpses of it. Someday we shall see and know a city which will ''exceed all that we can desire,'' but for now there are only glimpses. Thanks be to God.

Ascension of the Lord

Almighty God,
your Son Jesus Christ ascended to the throne of heaven
that he might rule over all things as Lord.
Keep the Church in the unity of the Spirit
and in the bond of his peace,
and bring the whole of creation
to worship at his feet,
who is alive and reigns with you and the Holy Spirit,
one God, now and for ever.

We cannot hope to understand a great mystery by defining and analysing it, but we still must strive to find some way of expressing what it means to us. Whatever else this moment in the life of Our Lord may have been, it is certainly the point at which a certain mode of his presence among us ended. Between his resurrection and this point there were moments of visible and tangible communication with the community of men and women who gathered around him. After this moment, which we call his ascension, that way of being present with them ceased. If we could have asked them whether they felt his presence among them had ended, they would have answered with a resounding no! All that had changed was a certain way of his being present.

"Jesus Christ ascended . . . that he might rule over all things as Lord." As we read the New Testament and watch the dawning of Christian belief, we see a process taking place. First of all there is a personal encounter between Jesus and certain men and women. Those men and women come to the conclusion that they have met a person in whom God is present, just as we today would say the same thing of an obviously holy life with whom we had come in contact. As time goes on they come to believe something more about Jesus. They begin to look on him as a kind of window through which they can see the nature of God.

More time goes by. We have moved beyond crucifixion and resurrection. Certain voices are now trying to express a most mysterious concept. John attempts it in the first chapter of his gospel, and Paul tries in the first chapter of his letter to the community in Colossae. It is the thought that somehow the window given them by Jesus' life and death and resurrection affords us a glimpse into the way the universe works. The ultimate love seen in him is the ultimate energy source in creation. His return from death by resurrection speaks of life rather than death being the ultimate meaning of existence. This is something of the meaning of the phrase, "that he might rule over all things."

If Jesus rules over all things or, in other words, gives meaning to all things, then the whole church most certainly comes under that rule. What might that mean at this time? Today Christian spirituality is a vast spectrum of different allegiances, methods, convictions, styles. It is absolutely necessary that we retain a vision of Jesus Christ as Lord of the church. It is paramount that we see Our Lord as the very essence of the church, rather than seeing as the essence its organization, its activities, its problems, its personalities, its ongoing existence in time and history. All such things are extremely real and important and undeniable. It is right that we should give allegiance and energy and dedication to the life of the church in the world of our time, but we must never see these things as its essence.

"Keep the Church in the unity of the Spirit and in the bond of his peace." Only if we acknowledge the lordship of Christ at the heart of all that the church tries to do and be, will we be able to deal with the otherwise utter humanity of the church. Our spirits will be broken without the grace of Our Lord's Holy Spirit. Without the acknowledgement of his lordship, there will be no bond to keep us faithful or to bridge the many gulfs in Christian vision and Christian intentions. With Christ we possess such a Spirit and such a bond. Thanks be to God.

Seventh Sunday of Easter

Almighty God,
you have exalted your only Son Jesus Christ
with great triumph to your kingdom in heaven.
Mercifully give us faith to know
that, as he promised,
he abides with us on earth to the end of time;
who is alive and reigns with you and the Holy Spirit,
one God, now and for ever.

In the very moment of Our Lord's final withdrawing of his physical presence, that moment in the gospel which we call the Ascension, something very significant is reported. The attention of the assembled men and women is drawn upward. They are standing there looking up. While they are frozen in that attitude, they are conscious of being addressed by a very corrective and challenging question. They are asked, "Why stand ye here gazing up into heaven?" The effect of the question is to release them from immobility, and they turn back to the city and the future that lies ahead.

This collect, while not asking that question again, is making sure that its message is not forgotten. Two things are said very clearly about Our Lord. He is beyond us, but he is also among us. It is most important that we keep these two realities in balance. That is the heart of what this collect is saying.

"You have exalted . . . Jesus Christ . . . to your kingdom in heaven." We are being told something extremely important about our own humanity, something that western Christianity has not remembered as well as eastern Orthodox Christianity. It is the realization that when God in Christ descended to inhabit our humanity in his incarnation, God in Christ also exalted our humanity in his resurrection and ascension. In spite of all the darkness in us, in spite of the terrible things we are capable of, our humanity has been lifted to the heights of God by Our Lord's divinity living in human flesh among us.

We cannot repeat too often the central Christian theme that the things we say of Jesus Christ are not applicable merely to one human life in a certain time and place. While that is certainly true, Christianity also teaches that the divine inhabited the whole of human nature, not just the human nature of one individual. Perhaps because this point is so central to Christian faith, it needs to be said again in a slightly different way. Although we believe that the divine nature entered into a single human nature, Jesus of Nazareth, Christian faith also believes that because the divine nature entered into that specific human nature, all of human nature was changed, lifted, touched by a light or a grace which is eternally within it.

Why dwell on this? Because it means that human nature, flawed though it may be, can be the instrument of God in history. Human gifts, insights, thought, intentions, creativity can all be used by God to form the future. This is not because of us but because of God in us.

It follows then that our vocation as Christians is to work and serve and create in the world in which we find ourselves. If our humanity has been touched by the presence of God through Our Lord's living of our humanity, then he is in and through all we do in his name. He is among us. In the deepest sense of the words, Our Lord is *in the world*. He is not isolated in the past as a wonderful memory. He is not isolated in thought as a wonderful concept. He is not isolated in a mysterious level of reality we call heaven. In the words of the collect, ''he abides with us on earth to the end of time.'' What then is wonderfully true of us is that we are the people of Our Lord. We are Our Lord's instruments, our Lord's companions, our Lord's fellow workers in the formation of the world. God, while having no illusions about us, has, thank God, an extraordinary amount of confidence in us, considerably more than we ourselves sometimes have. Thanks be to God.

The Day of Pentecost

Almighty and everliving God,
who fulfilled the promises of Easter
by sending us your Holy Spirit
and opening to every race and nation
the way of life eternal,
keep us in the unity of your Spirit,
that every tongue may tell of your glory;
through Jesus Christ our Lord,
who lives and reigns with you and the Holy Spirit,
one God, now and for ever.

Our Lord Jesus Christ encountered his first disciples in three different ways. While the ways of the encounter differed, those disciples never doubted that it was always the same Lord whom they were encountering. They met him first as you and I would meet anybody else. They would doubtless often retell the particular moment, whether it was by the shore or in the town or elsewhere. That kind of encounter was theirs for about three years, perhaps less. Their Lord was then brutally killed. After that, as we know, Our Lord met them again in various circumstances. However, we can tell, as they could, that there was a difference. It was as if Our Lord had moved on to another level of being but still retained the power to use the physical and temporal for his purposes. In this second kind of encounter, they and we refer to the Risen Lord.

There was a third way of encountering him. There came a time when his visible presence was finally withdrawn and they awaited the next event. When it came, it took them by storm. It literally possessed them. It transformed them, energized them, inspired them, renewed them. The word we use for that event, the word *Pentecost*, has become almost synonymous with inspiration, transformation, and renewal. When it first happened to those early disciples, they realized that Our Lord ''had fulfilled the promises of Easter by sending his Holy Spirit.'' From then on they realized that he was literally among them, in their own selves, in their actions, in their relationships, in their gathered life as a community bearing his name and choosing him as its Lord.

The event said another thing to them. They began to suspect something that would take them many years to realize fully. Was what had happened around those villages and that lakeside bigger than their own world and even bigger than Judaism? At first, it was a concept so mind-boggling that they did not grasp it. Full realization was to be a long and painful struggle, and the resolution of that struggle was not to come for many years. To this day we have difficulty realizing that Jesus Christ is universal.

There are many disagreements among us as to how Our Lord should be spoken of as universal, how we should try to confess him before the other great religions of the world. But there is no disagreement as to whether the things he said and the events which took place around him are of universal significance. If it be true that a man lives a life of extraordinary moral power, dies a completely undeserved death before which he prays for his murderers, and after death is so clearly present among his friends that they speak of him in terms of the visible and the tangible, then those things are significant for every human being on this planet. We may want to impose those realities on others, or we may have no intention of doing so. That is not the point. It is still true that if these things are true, they cannot be of less than universal significance.

The question remains to this day. How do we tell this story? In the words of the collect, how may ''every tongue tell of his glory''? However much we may want the unity of the Spirit, it is highly unlikely that it will be granted within history. We will always differ as to how we tell of Our Lord, how we commend him to others, how we speak of what means so much to ourselves. There is, however, one thing about which there can be no disunity. It is the way whereby we live him. That is the acid test of whether his Spirit is within us. How do we live so that our daily lives witness to him, at best with a minimum of words? Not one of us is prevented from that kind of witness. Thanks be to God.

Trinity Sunday

Father, we praise you:
through your Word and Holy Spirit you created all things.
You reveal your salvation in all the world
by sending to us Jesus Christ, the Word made flesh.
Through your Holy Spirit
you give us a share in your life and love.
Fill us with the vision of your glory,
that we may always serve and praise you,
Father, Son, and Holy Spirit,
one God, for ever and ever.

The mysterious reality which Christians call the Holy Trinity is so complex and rich in meaning that it is impossible to explain with any one analogy. Perhaps that should not surprise us. After all, the teaching we call the Trinity is trying to describe God. We are bound to fail, but we try because we must. There is something in our humanity that wishes to understand even though we know we never will.

The nearest we can get is to describe what God does. That at least is more within our grasp than the impossibility of describing what God is. However, there is one aspect of God which this collect communicates immediately and with utter simplicity. It tells us that whatever God is and however far the divine nature must remain beyond our understanding, there is one glorious word which describes God's relationship to us. The collect's first word is *Father*.

Today we have many questions about how best to express the love which is contained in that word. As with all words about God, it is unable to contain the reality. To say that God is father, for instance, is not to deny that God is mother. In the end both words fail us. What we are trying to express is the idea of life and love being totally given that we identify with the best of human parenthood.

Having begun with this beautiful and deceptively simple statement about God, the collect then tells us three things which God does. God creates. God reveals. God shares with us.

"Through your word and Holy Spirit you created all things." Just as our spirits are creative, so is the Spirit of God. The difference is beyond description, but the analogy is helpful. At this moment your spirit and mine are together creating a communication of ideas and insights between us. But the real source of that communication is the Holy Spirit, of which your spirit and mine are only pathetic and faint echoes or reflections. Again, you and I are communicating in words. We both know how very powerful words are for good or ill, but when we speak of the Word of God, we mean something infinitely different. We might say that the difference lies in what happens when we say a word and when God says a word. When we say the word *star*, all that comes into being is the image of a star in our own mind and in the mind of the person who hears us. When God says the word *star*, there, actual and real, is a star, hanging in space, blazing in the heavens, enriching a galaxy!

"You reveal your salvation . . . by sending to us . . . the Word made flesh." Christian faith believes that the most significant word ever spoken by God is the Word that took human form, Our Lord Jesus Christ. That Word, as with all God's creative words, not only spoke to us of God but *was* God to us and for us.

"You give us a share in your life and love." All through the Bible something immensely affirming of our humanity is being said to us again and again. Every time God wishes something done in the world, the first thing God does is to search out a man or a woman through whom to get it done. That person's response is all important to God. God listens for the single word *yes* from human lips when God offers us a task. By this we realize that we human beings have a great vocation. We are called to be the co-creators of the world with God. The degree to which we live with this "vision of God's glory" is the degree to which we will have grace to "serve and praise" God. Thanks be to God.

Sunday between 5 and 11 June, Proper 10

O God,
you have assured the human family of eternal life
through Jesus Christ our Saviour.
Deliver us from the death of sin
and raise us to new life in him,
who lives and reigns with you and the Holy Spirit,
one God, now and for ever.

As we look at the opening sentence of this collect, we hear a great claim being made. It is suggested that the events around the life of Jesus of Nazareth are significant not merely for Christians but for the whole human family. The words imply nothing less than this. We claim that God has "assured the human family of eternal life through Jesus Christ our Saviour."

We need to face this statement and all that it implies for contemporary Christian thinking. That thinking is very ambivalent about the consequences, in Christian life and activity, of assuming that there are universal elements implicit in the life of Jesus Christ. Some Christians feel that Christianity must confront other great religious traditions with at best their incompleteness and at worst their downright error. Other Christians feel equally strongly that we have no right to do anything like this, that we must acknowledge the particular truths and integrity of the great Ways or religions, and that each, including Christianity, represents one way of seeking the mystery we call God. Each one of us will find ourselves standing at some point in this spectrum of attitudes.

But something remains to be dealt with that is not easy

to ignore. It can be expressed fairly simply, but its solution is far from simple. If we believe that in the life of Jesus of Nazareth we have indeed been given a window into the nature of God, then we will quite naturally wish to share the insights shown to us by that window. It will of course be quite reasonable for other great faiths to wish to share with us the insights they have found through the window into God which their tradition has given them.

If we truly believe that in the death of Jesus Christ we are seeing an event of eternal significance for the meaning of our humanity, and if we truly believe that after that death Jesus of Nazareth passed to a level of being from which he was able to communicate with us in a tangible and visible way, then we have something which we simply must communicate to the rest of the human family. In that sense *mission*, to use a word many Christians have become uncomfortable with, is not something aggressive and insensitive which implies the dismissal of other great faiths, but is something by which we wish to share what we truly believe to be of universal significance.

For those of us who are Christian, the collect goes on to express our prayer that we may be delivered and raised by Our Lord. What do we mean by these things? What is the death of sin? It means that we can live out our lives in such a way that they end in a terrible cul-de-sac of the spirit, where in the deepest sense of the expression, we are dead. We may be smiling and jogging and driving our car and getting on with our profession, but we will have died inside. The degree to which our own will and our own self is paramount is the degree to which we die spiritually. The degree to which you and I offer our whole self and will to Our Lord is the degree to which we stumble on a new way of being alive — ''new life,'' as the collect calls it. The most important aspect of all this is that the choice is ours. Thanks be to God.

Sunday between 12 and 18 June, Proper 11

Almighty God,
without you we are not able to please you.
Mercifully grant that your Holy Spirit
may in all things direct and rule our hearts;
through Jesus Christ our Lord,
who is alive and reigns with you and the Holy Spirit,
one God, now and for ever.

"Almighty God, without you we are not able to please you." Like many of the collects, this prayer is a very old friend. We have been saying it generation after generation for centuries, and it is a particularly beautiful expression of the eternal love affair between humanity and God. That opening sentence could be said by a lover about his or her beloved. Without you I am not able to please you.

It is easy to forget that there is a great gift which God gives each one of us merely by being present in our lives. It is the same gift that others in our lives give us when by their very existence they provide us with a focus beyond the self. Without such a focus we die spiritually; the self becomes a kind of black hole. Black holes in the universe are areas from which nothing can escape. Everything centres on the hole. Everything is drawn into it. Given half a chance, the self within us can become such a consuming, demanding tyrant. To possess God as a reality in our lives is to have a way out of this tyranny.

To possess God is to have an even greater gift than any human relationship, although one realizes that it is through our human relationships that the love of God is mediated to us. But to have the will of God as counterpoint to our own will and self is to have an ultimate focus for our lives. No other relationship will call us farther, inspire us more deeply, forgive us as totally, accept us as utterly. The love of God is the ultimate love affair, as many great souls have discovered, and as most ordinary souls like our own discover in tantalizing moments of spiritual discernment, only to lose again.

"Mercifully grant that your Holy Spirit may in all things direct and rule our hearts." Because we know our need of God, we ask for God's indwelling in us. But the request is made for a more complex reason too. We know that we will not always feel the need of God. Large areas of our lives, great lengths of time in our lives, go by when our sense of God's presence is weak and even nonexistent. Knowing this we use a moment of nearness to God, such as saying this collect, to ask God to do what we cannot do, to keep the relationship strong and real and rich. We know in those rare moments of spiritual clarity that our whole relationship with God depends on God. If it depended on our weak and wayward will and emotions and commitment, then the outlook would be poor indeed! There is a very old and simple prayer which sums up this whole area of spiritual experience. "O God, I shall be very busy this day. I shall forget thee. Do not thou forget me."

We might think for a moment of the meaning of the words *direct and rule our hearts* in the relationship between God and a human spirit. We must always realize that God will direct and rule only to the extent that it is our wish that this be done. Saint John gives us the unforgettable image of Our Lord and the Father knocking at the door of a human life. In that image everything depends on the willingness of the human life to open the door from the inside. God is not an invading God, directing and ruling as one who brooks no other opinion or wish or authority. God is a God who responds to invitations. If I truly wish direction and a rule other than the tyranny of my own desires and wishes, then I will receive them. Thanks be to God.

Sunday between 19 and 25 June, Proper 12

O God our defender,
storms rage about us and cause us to be afraid.
Rescue your people from despair,
deliver your sons and daughters from fear,
and preserve us all from unbelief;
through your Son, Jesus Christ our Lord,
who lives and reigns with you and the Holy Spirit,
one God, now and ever.

"O God our defender." This is a very ancient image for God, used often in the psalms and Christian hymns. Is it an illusion, a symptom of the dependency of which many accuse religious faith? It can be. There can be an unreal and neurotic dependency on God, a clinging to God as a magic protection against things we fear. There can be the conviction, because of some virtue arising out of our faith in God, some reward that comes to us because of our faith, that things which happen to others will not happen to us.

Does the phrase "O God our defender" suggest an illusory image of God? Not always, not if it means that possessing the reality of God in one's life is indeed a defence against many enemies, most of them within our deepest being. The collect mentions those things against which God can be our defender.

"Storms rage about us and cause us to be afraid." We live in a time of many storms. They rage at every level of contemporary human experience. They arise particularly because we are being asked by God to live in one of the stormiest periods of history. Storms of change are thundering about us and making every facet of life exhausting and insecure. Also battering us are the inner storms of all the consequences of that change — insecurity, anxiety, complexity. There is the terrible feeling that nobody knows the answers. This is perfectly true! Our response to all the turmoil about us is a deep and widespread fear. Very often this fear emerges as various angers and resentments, which in turn can bedevil our relationships and bring about a considerable amount of loneliness.

"They cause us to be afraid." There is indeed a great deal of fear about many things in modern life — fear about ourselves and our ability to cope, about our children, about job insecurity, inflation, retirement. Children have many fears about the future of society. Youth has fears about the declining job market. In this collect we acknowledge those fears, and that in itself may be very healing.

Notice that immediately after admitting fear, we speak of ourselves as "your people." The implication is that we are not alone in what we have to face. If we are prepared to see ourselves as a people drawn together by more than formal ties of church membership, if the congregation is prepared to be a place of trust, of mutual helping, of relationships, then we are not alone with our fears. And if it is true that we are not alone with them, we can begin to deal with them.

The three particular demons we wrestle with form an interesting sequence in the collect. They are despair, fear, unbelief. The collect suggests that those are the real enemies, the ones we really have to watch. To despair means that everything is really in danger. There is an old story that the only enemy Moses really feared in the wilderness was that the people would despair. He knew that if that happened, the journey was over. Fear can have the effect of immobilizing us, taking from us the ability to think clearly about our situation. Fear can emerge in anger against others and against God. Fear can trigger resentment toward others because we have projected our fear and anger on to them. The third dangerous enemy is to be without a belief system in our lives. The very possession of Christian faith can be our most real and strong defence against this formidable line-up of inner enemies. In the gift of faith given to us, God becomes indeed and in truth "our defender." Thanks be to God.

Sunday between 26 June and 2 July, Proper 13

Almighty God,
you have taught us through your Son
that love fulfils the law.
May we love you with all our heart,
all our soul, all our mind, and all our strength,
and may we love our neighbour as ourselves;
through Jesus Christ our Lord,
who lives and reigns with you and the Holy Spirit,
one God, now and for ever.

There is an old story of an eastern ruler who insisted that his philosophers find the absolute kernel of all wisdom. The story goes through many stages. First they brought their findings in a set of books, only to be asked for a single book, then a single page, and finally a single sentence. The sentence they produced was, "This too shall pass." Such was their ultimate wisdom about life.

The opening lines of this collect are doing the same thing for Christian faith. They are responding to our wish to state in a single sentence what the life of Jesus Christ taught us. The answer is a very much more creative and inspiring one than the answer the ancients gave their ruler. The collect tells us that God taught us through Our Lord that "love fulfils the law."

What does it mean in ordinary everyday living to say this? It means that whatever else we do, we love. That of course is very much easier to say than to do. It does not mean that we are always what others would wish us to be. It does not mean that we cannot be angry, assign blame, criticize, or call people to account for their actions. To do these things does not for a moment mean that we do not love them. Indeed there are times when not to do these things is to fail to act lovingly.

To love means to have the best interest of the other at heart — nothing more, nothing less. The direction of love is always toward the other. That is precisely the essence of Our Lord's earthly life. Even when the disciples try to prevent it because of their concern for him, he will still expend himself. He is on his last trip to Jerusalem, turning up the hill from Jericho on the last lap, when Bartimaeus' voice refuses to be stilled. Even then, when Our Lord had every reason to serve himself and his needs and his own very real fears, he gives his healing energies to the blind man. It is typical of Jesus. To mention one example serves only to bring others to mind without effort.

This then is our vocation as Christians, to be like Our Lord. It is so simple to say and so daunting a challenge. Yet the simple statement is utterly true. We are called to be like Our Lord. "Let this mind be in you," said Paul, referring to the mind of Our Lord.

The collect also speaks of our minds, demanding that we love with them. To love with the mind is to inject discipline into our loving. To love with the mind is to refrain from acting with a seeming love that is actually no more than sentimentality, and is therefore not love at all. To love without the mind is to betray love for something lesser.

"May we love with all our heart." The collect speaks of loving both God and neighbour. To love God without loving neighbour is something less than love. It can conceivably be religion, but it is a loveless and unreal religion. There is nothing more unattractive than an intense piety devoid of love.

"May we love with all." Notice how the commandment sings the word *all* like a chorus. On whatever level of our being we love, we are to love with all of our commitment. Why? Because we follow a Lord who loved utterly and passionately. Thanks be to God.

Sunday between 3 and 9 July, Proper 14

Almighty God,
your Son Jesus Christ has taught us
that what we do for the least of your children
we do also for him.
Give us the will to serve others
as he was the servant of all,
who gave up his life and died for us,
but lives and reigns with you and the Holy Spirit,
one God, now and for ever.

As this collect begins with the phrase "the least of your children" it is linking us with two themes in the gospel. The first is the great vision of the last judgment in Matthew where we see the king separating those who have served others from those who have not. At one point the king expresses gratitude for help given to him on various occasions — in sickness, in prison, hungry, and so on. The surprised recipients of the king's thanks ask when that was. The king says simply, "As you did it to one of the least of these my brethren, you did it unto me." That episode echoes in the lines of this collect.

The second echo is of a moment when Our Lord took a child, set the child on his knee, turned to his disciples, and told them that unless they were prepared to become like a child, they would not see the kingdom that he constantly spoke to them about.

Deep within the Christian tradition, emerging in countless stories, many of them in the lives of the saints, is the theme of the Christ in disguise. The theme occurs in many cultures, sometimes in the shape of the king or prince or princess who walks disguised as a beggar. Almost always the disguise is that of the poor or the injured or the simple in mind. But what is easily missed in the stories is that the royal person adopts the disguise and walks among others to discover wisdom.

The theme has come down to us in Christian faith as a constant reminder that if we wish to see the Christ of our time, we would be wise to look in places where many would never dream of looking. We should look where there is weakness of some kind, where there is poverty, where people have been in some way dismissed out of the mainstream of life, where they have been marginalized. This is really the point of that whole twenty-fifth chapter of the gospel according to Matthew. In those areas we serve the Christ who is in disguise.

What has that got to do with becoming like a child? To be able to think in these terms at all we have to invert most of the values of our culture. Our deepest instincts are to look at the centre of things where power, activity, affluence, initiative, control seem to be. These are the things of the ''adult'' world. There is a sense in which poverty, weakness, seeming ineffectiveness, spontaneity are the things of our ''child'' world. Christian faith points out to us that within the latter world there are values which our adult one sorely needs.

In using the words *adult* and *child* we are not speaking literally of adults and children. We are trying to express two levels of understanding, two ways of seeing reality which remain in us all our lives unless one, usually the child, gets crushed out of existence by our culture or neglect. The sophistication of our adult world needs the innocence of our child world to pierce it and show its short-comings. The faith and trust of our child world is needed in the mistrust and cynicism of our adult world. To return to the idea of seeing the Christ in disguise is not easy for our adult eyes. It is the gift of childhood to see through things in a kind of magic way. We err if we dismiss this ability as the fancy of our early years. We very badly need to keep the gift of looking through the surface of things and seeing the hidden truths within. If we do preserve that gift, we will retain the ability to see Our Lord himself in areas of life all too easily dismissed with terminology such as ''social problems'' and ''political issues.'' Thanks be to God.

Sunday between 10 and 16 July, Proper 15

Almighty God,
you have made us for yourself,
and our hearts are restless
until they find their rest in you.
May we find peace in your service,
and in the world to come, see you face to face;
through Jesus Christ our Lord,
who lives and reigns with you and the Holy Spirit,
one God, now and for ever.

This collect contains an insight into the meaning of human life which, once grasped, offers us a pearl of great price. We human beings are always asking questions of the deepest meaning about our lives. As we toss those questions around in our reflective moments it is very easy to miss certain great responses which are part of our rich Christian heritage.

For instance, consider the response in the catechism to the question, ''Who gave you this name?'' We reply, ''My Godfathers and Godmothers in my baptism, wherein I was made a member of Christ, the child of God, and an inheritor of the kingdom of heaven.'' Here is a Christian response to the questions about our lives. This is who I am. I am *the* child of God, a particular and unique creation. I am a member of a reality far greater than myself, the body of Jesus Christ, and I have a hope and a destiny, the kingdom of heaven.

The opening lines of this collect are another great and famous response to the questions about the meaning of one's life. The words themselves come from one of the great souls of Christian history, Augustine of Hippo. He lived in a tumultuous and changing age. He would know instinctively what it is like to be Christian at the end of the twentieth century. His Christian journey to faith was far from easy, but when he finally said his great yes to Our Lord, he found peace and meaning which he never again lost. He became one of the spiritual giants of the whole Christian family through time. Reflecting about his relationship with God, he one day shared this thought which will never die. ''O God, you have made us for yourself, and our hearts are restless until they find their rest in you.''

The human heart is a restless thing. We all know that. Perhaps its physical restlessness is an image of the restlessness throughout our whole being. The heart is always pumping the great river of our life through our bodies. It is never at rest from the moment we are born to the moment we die. Like that heart our being is restless. We search for the meaning of things. We want to discover more things. We search for relationships. We search for knowledge. We need constant change. We search for love, both to give and to receive.

Augustine realized the single great truth of that restlessness. Among all that we search for there is only one thing we really want to find. Paradoxically that thing is not a thing! We are really in search of God. The creature searches for the creator. The homeless one in us searches for our true home. We are creatures in a kind of exile from our true state, and we long to recover that state. Nobody has written more hauntingly about this sense of exile in us than C.S. Lewis, as he tells of our lifelong searching for the strange mysterious quality he names *joy*. By that word he means far more than mere happiness. For Lewis, joy is that state of being in which we glimpse — for we can only get glimpses now — the beauty and the peace and the presence which is God. Only then, as Augustine would say, is our restlessness quieted, and, such is our human nature, it is even then quieted only for a time.

"May we find peace in your service." The end of our restlessness does not mean passivity. It means we can serve better because we know who we are and what we are for. We are no longer fragmented. We are focused. Furthermore, when we have a clearer vision of who we are and what we are for, we have a clearer vision of God. Thanks be to God.

Sunday between 17 and 23 July, Proper 16

Almighty God,
your Son has opened for us
a new and living way into your presence.
Give us pure hearts and constant wills
to worship you in spirit and in truth;
through Jesus Christ our Lord,
who lives and reigns with you and the Holy Spirit,
one God, now and for ever.

In many stories which we sometimes tell our children or read ourselves, a certain journey will be taken. Sometimes the travellers will come to a place where the road is blocked or the river has rapids or a great crevasse has opened. One person will become the heroic figure who risks perhaps life itself to clear the way. That person either finds a way around or else climbs to get help, but somehow the journey continues because of the action of one person.

Christian faith is full of such images as this, a result of countless attempts to express what the journey of faith means and who Our Lord Jesus Christ really is. This collect images Our Lord as the person who clears the way that is blocked and makes it possible for the Christian journey to continue.

Human life is created to return to its creator, The day you and I are baptized we begin this journey. It is a strange and mysterious journey, and yet at the same time it passes through the most familiar places in our lives. We are taking it every waking and sleeping moment although we may not be aware of it, or even acknowledge it. Along the way we gain all sorts of companions — the people who love us, and many who do not! Those who teach us (and they are far more numerous than we realize), those whom we help, and those whom we wrong and hurt. There are those with whom we live in total intimacy perhaps for many years, and those among whom we may choose to worship. We have in fact a great multitude of companions on the Christian journey, just as we are companion to many others.

But there come times when the journey we are taking brings us to great blockages. Our journey as a Christian seems to be at an end. The block may be for many reasons. Some are of our own making, but not all. There can be an avalanche of tragedy which breaks our capacity to go on with the journey. There can be floods of fear and anxiety. There can be great crevasses or cave-ins of depression. There can be dreadful mistakes made, which seem to bring down the world upon us. There can be mountains of guilt which suddenly loom ahead with no visible pass through them.

Christian faith points to the companion we have been given. Many times in Christian prayer over the centuries Our Lord is named simply as Friend. We do well to remember that lovely simple image of him. The single most important thing about this friend is that he has already made this journey. He has been through this threatening stretch of countryside. He has climbed this mountain pass. He has forded this flood. He has scaled this cliff. He has faced this threat. He has felt this ghastly fear, he has experienced this sense of desperate loneliness. He has done all this, and he has completed the journey.

''Your Son has opened for us a new and living way.'' There is great encouragement in this collect. It says to us that there is a way other than the way which has become blocked for us. There is a way that is not blocked because the grace of Our Lord has cleared it. That way is offered to us. Part of that way leads through territory we take far too much for granted, the territory called worship. The collect is telling us that this is territory where we should expect to encounter Our Lord. Perhaps there cannot be vivid encounters always, but if we are open to the possibility, there will be some. Such an encounter with Our Lord in worship can enable us to walk out into a world where the way that seemed blocked is once again open for us. Thanks be to God.

Sunday between 24 and 30 July, Proper 17

O God,
the protector of all who trust in you,
without whom nothing is strong, nothing is holy,
increase and multiply upon us your mercy,
that with you as our ruler and guide,
we may so pass through things temporal,
that we lose not the things eternal;
through Jesus Christ our Lord,
who lives and reigns with you and the Holy Spirit,
one God, for ever and ever.

"O God, the protector of all who trust in you." There is a very wrong kind of religion which can use statements like this in very unreal and unhealthy ways. But the collect is making no impossible claims. This is not a facile assurance that if one believes in God then life will be without pain or difficulty. To claim this is a lie, and to try to get others to believe it is gross exploitation. We have only to look at Our Lord himself to see how untrue this is. Christian faith is not a device for protecting oneself and one's loved ones from life. It is a resource to assist us in coming to terms with what life brings, and in handling those things creatively and gracefully.

"Those who trust." The operative word in this sentence is *trust*. The ability to trust is itself a kind of armour, a source of energy and resilience. Trust is a gift of God. It is a protection against being overcome by such things as faintheartedness, cynicism, doubt — all those strong demons which can overcome us. We have not said that trust can protect us from these things. They arrive in every life and make

their onslaughts. But trust can protect us from being overcome by them.

"Without whom nothing is strong, nothing is holy."
Many things are very strong indeed without God. Many
kinds of evil are incredibly strong, and those who perpe-
trate them are very far from God. What then is being said
here? The strong and the holy are together. Nothing merely
good in its intentions is strong without God. Human intention and human dedication wearies and disperses. This is
not betrayal but normal human limitation. There needs to
be a source beyond the human yet mediated through the
human.

"Increase and multiply upon us your mercy." English
has tended to link mercy in our minds with pity and
leniency. To speak of the mercy of God is much richer.
Mercy is a kind of shorthand description of the attitude of
a loving creator to the creature. It is our belief in that mercy
that convinces us that God is essentially for us rather than
against us. We could substitute the word *grace* for mercy
here. But for what purpose do we ask this mercy?

"That with you as our ruler and guide." It is easy to
forget how foreign this statement is to our age. We have
a thousand therapies offering guidance for every part of life.
We have countless rulers making ultimate demands on our
time and allegiance. Consumerism is such a ruler — com-
forting, rewarding, insatiable. The longing for total national
security can rule, demandingly and expensively. There are
dark rulers such as drugs. They offer peace and power, but
their final gift is death.

"We may so pass through things temporal, that we lose
not the things eternal." A prayer for the very core of our
lives. We must of course pass through temporal things. Even
Our Lord chose to do that. Time and space, this fragile and
transitory house of ours which can be both sweet and bit-
ter, liberating and imprisoning, is where we must do our
living. But we must never succumb to the illusion that this
is all there is. The temporal is not evil. It only becomes a

demon when we allow it to hide the eternal, when we allow our agenda to masquerade as *the* agenda, and our wonderful fascinating unreality to hide God's powerful and grace-giving reality. The petition of this collect is that we may be given grace that this does not happen. Thanks be to God.

Sunday between 31 July and 6 August, Proper 18

Almighty God,
your Son Jesus Christ fed the hungry
with the bread of his life
and the word of his kingdom.
Renew your people with your heavenly grace,
and in all our weakness
sustain us by your true and living bread,
who lives and reigns with you and the Holy Spirit,
one God, now and for ever.

Earlier in this century, some twenty to twenty-five years ago, the church on this continent passed through a period when the church's vocation and, for that matter, the whole Christian faith, went through a great agonizing. The church agonized about the validity of the spiritual. Was prayer anything more than an expression of need and childish dependency? Was worship any more than a gathering of like-minded people doing something that gave them pleasure? Was there any necessity for an institutional church? In fact, was there any validity to the whole spiritual enterprise? Was it not time to drop all the traditional mystery and spirituality of Christian faith and concentrate on its practical application in society. Such was the nature of much of the questioning.

We now realize, with the wisdom that hindsight can always give, that it was a false and unnecessary agonizing. The issue was not whether we should pray or work, or whether we should worship or serve. Many centuries before our own, the great insight of Benedict had recognized that we would always have to be aware of separating these two activities. The Benedictine motto was "*Laborare est orare*" — To work is to pray. Christian life, if it is to remain healthy and creative, needs to recognize that the human spirit must have a source of spirituality to give the energy and motivation and grace to serve in the world. Very often in the past, even when men and women were greatly dedicated to various social causes, the dedication began to flag if there was not a source of grace beyond the self.

"Jesus Christ fed the hungry with the bread of his life and the word of his kingdom." In a single sentence the collect brings together the two aspects of Our Lord's work. Jesus never offered a detached and unreal spirituality. He never denied that bread was not necessary. Again and again when there is hunger, he responds with total practicality. He offers food. When there is a need of physical healing, he begins by offering physical healing. But Our Lord never stops there. He moves into the deeper needs of the situation and offers something at another level. He heals paralysis but then moves into the possible reasons for the paralysis. He heals the body and then the spirit. He feeds physical hunger and then responds to the presence of a spiritual hunger.

The climax of this way in which Our Lord always communicates on two levels is his institution of the Eucharist. As he holds a piece of bread, he speaks of his own body and issues an invitation that all of us may become part of that body. He holds up bread both as a physical object and as a spiritual symbol. In effect he is telling us that it must always be both. Christian faith is about the material and the spiritual, physical bread and spiritual bread.

The collect asks simply that we never forget this. Part of "all our weakness" as Christians is to reduce Christian faith to a spirituality that is merely spiritual. We may ask what else a spirituality can be? There is indeed something better. It can and must be sacramental, both reaching for

God and rooted in the world, both praying and serving, both worshipping and working — always true, not just as mental or even spiritual concepts, but true in a living way, applied in the comings and goings of real life. We can sum it up in a sentence. A Christian gives physical and spiritual bread. Never is it either/or. It is both/and. Thanks be to God.

Sunday between 7 and 13 August, Proper 19

Almighty God,
you sent your Holy Spirit
to be the life and light of your Church.
Open our hearts to the riches of your grace,
that we may bring forth the fruit of the Spirit
in love, joy, and peace;
through Jesus Christ our Lord,
who is alive and reigns with you and the Holy Spirit,
one God, now and for ever.

"Almighty God, you sent your Holy Spirit." Christians always look back to certain realities. Those realities are the events in the beginning of the Christian story which made all the ensuing centuries possible. But in looking back we Christians do not believe that the reality of the event is only a past reality. In the same breath as we say that God sent the Holy Spirit, we also say that God sends the Holy Spirit. The past event is not limited to the past. The only thing that is past is the beginning of the Spirit's coming. That Spirit, we believe, will continue to come until the end of time. That is exactly what we mean when we say that the Spirit was sent to be the life and light of the church. We are not thinking of that sending as a blaze of wonderful light and life which blinded us for a long-ago moment, or even a decade or a generation, but a light and a life which men and women today can experience as Christians.

"Open our hearts to the riches of your grace." One of the obstinate illusions of western Christianity is the attitude of many to the Holy Spirit. Instinctively many Christians think of the Holy Spirit of God as something which must be pursued, searched for, run to earth, captured, and brought into our lives! For many Christians their relationship with God's Holy Spirit is a kind of big game hunt! The weapons used in this hunt are the weapons of piety. Prayer, worship, Bible reading, receiving the sacrament, personal piety, retreats — all are used. The irony is that none of these things is wrong. Every one of them is a valuable part of Christian formation. But there is a sense in which none of them is necessary to the pursuit of the Holy Spirit because the Holy Spirit, far from running away from us, is within us! No matter how often we are told this, we find it difficult to make it a natural part of our understanding of the relationship between Our Lord and ourselves.

That is why it is important to look at the words in this collect, "Open our hearts." Notice that nothing is said about opening our hearts to find or to search for the riches of grace. The riches of grace to which we need to be open are already in us, freely and joyously given by God as the waters of baptism splashed over our bodies. Grace is in us. Our Lord is within us. "The kingdom," as he said, "is within."

There is an old story of Rabindranath Tagore about a man who lived on the side of a valley in a small house. Early one morning he looked and saw across the valley a golden door. All day he journeyed down the hillside, across the floor of the valley, and up the opposite side. It was evening when he arrived. There was only a ruined hut with a broken window. He looked everywhere for the golden door, but it had disappeared. He was quite certain this was the area in which he had seen it in the morning. Finally, exhausted and deeply disappointed, he gave up the search and headed down the hillside for the long journey home. It was only then that he looked across the valley in the direction of his own small house and saw a shimmering golden door. The spirituality of many Christians is not unlike that man, searching desperately in myriad directions for what lies within themselves, longing for them to discover its riches.

''That we may bring forth the fruit of the Spirit.'' Our task is not so much to go looking for the Holy Spirit as to realize we possess it. We need to realize that we possess it because only then can we begin to live it, to use it, to draw on it. Thanks be to God.

Sunday between 14 and 20 August, Proper 20

Almighty God,
you have broken the tyranny of sin
and sent into our hearts the Spirit of your Son.
Give us grace to dedicate our freedom to your service,
that all people may know the glorious liberty
of the children of God;
through Jesus Christ our Lord,
who lives and reigns with you and the Holy Spirit,
one God, now and for ever.

Again and again the Christian faith tries to tell us something of supreme importance about our Lord Jesus Christ. What we are being told is always essentially the same thing — how he has become Saviour and Lord for us. We are told many times and in many different ways because the truth of Our Lord's life, death, and resurrection is so deep and so many-faceted that there is no one way of expressing it. In this collect we hear that eternal truth expressed in a particular image or story. We see Our Lord as liberator.

''Almighty God, you have broken the tyranny of sin.'' The picture or the story we are given portrays human nature as in prison, the prisoner of a tyrant. The tyrant is what the Bible calls sin. It is important to remember that the prisoner is in prison through his own choice! When our human nature performed the act of disobedience which landed us in this prison of sin, it did not of course foresee or intend the result. The tyrant, sin or Satan, lied to our human nature and told us that our act of disobedience would result in a tremendous sense of freedom, the very opposite of prison. But here we are in prison nevertheless.

The Bible tells this story as if it were a single event in the remote past. But the same story can be told in the present, in human nature today, and in our very own lives. We are free beings and we exercise that freedom of choice a thousand times a day. But there is another sense in which we feel ourselves to be prisoners of what we would tend to call our humanity. That humanity which we share is a wonderful and creative thing, and yet at the same time it is a wounded and flawed thing. It is capable of choosing good, but it is also capable of choosing evil. At other times it intends good but because of its flawed moral vision, it brings about evil, and then we have to wrestle with remorse and guilt. Saddest of all, there are those times when we want to do good and we are drawn to do evil. In this sense we are prisoners of our own flawed nature.

Our Lord is Our Lord because we believe he did something about this. He came into our prison, into the prison of our human nature, and he transformed it. He lived our human nature as it could be lived if it were not a prison. He lived our human nature as it would be lived without sin. That is what this collect is telling us by using the image of the prisoner and the liberator.

To the degree that we identify our lives with his life, we can get out of prison. We can never leave entirely because the flaw in our human nature remains as long as we are human. But, to continue the prison metaphor, we can get out on parole. Our Lord can give us the grace to fight the battle that continually has to be fought with our self-will and its innate sinfulness. Our Lord can open our eyes to see our true situation. The tragedy is that very often human nature is blind to that true situation. Prison has become so normal that it is no longer seen to be prison, and, perhaps even sadder, there is no vision of a life of freedom. That is exactly the prayer in the second half of the collect. We are asking Our Lord to help us to realize that he has freed us from a tyrant within ourselves, that we have freedom to make new choices about our lives and our society, and that we can make those choices according to Our Lord's perfect will rather than our own sinful will. Thanks be to God.

Sunday between 21 and 27 August, Proper 21

Almighty God,
we are taught by your word
that all our doings without love are worth nothing.
Send your Holy Spirit and pour into our hearts
that most excellent gift of love,
the true bond of peace and of all virtue;
through Jesus Christ our Lord,
who lives and reigns with you and the Holy Spirit,
one God, now and for ever.

There is a moment in the New Testament when we look over Paul's shoulder as he writes the most difficult letter of his life. He writes to the Christian community in Corinth, and he is angry and frustrated because almost everything that could go wrong has gone wrong. There seems to be no sense of moral standards in Corinth and little sense of community. There comes a stage in the letter when Paul is listing the gifts that are worthwhile having. He goes through various gifts which need not concern us at the moment and then he says, "Now I will show you the best way of all," and launches into one of the most magnificent passages in the whole New Testament. His theme is love, and it is from that letter to Corinth that this collect takes its theme.

"All our doings without love are worth nothing." There are indeed many human gifts, and Paul himself had many of them. Ironically there were many human gifts in the Corinth community. It was a large, cosmopolitan, sophisticated city, the kind of place where there is a great deal of creativity, brilliance, imagination. It abounded in art and

144 Praying to the Lord of Life

philosophy. Life was mentally and emotionally very rich — in fact, overrich and inclining to the decadent. There were certain things Paul could detect underneath the veneer of sophistication. He could see a great deal of snobbery and elitism. It was quite obvious that there was much selfishness. There was very little social conscience. Sexual life was overintense and often perverse and unhealthy. The portrait of Corinth looks rather familiar to any urbanite of our time!

In the midst of all this, Paul insists that the most precious gift that any human being can possess is the capacity to love. It is more important than intellectual brilliance, which can be as cold as ice. It is better than being highly cultured, which can be so without a trace of humanity. Paul points out that even the gesture of giving to others can be carried out in a way devoid of love and real caring.

"The true bond of peace and of all virtue." Paul sees love not so much as one virtue among all the virtues, but as a surrounding reality whose presence changes any other thought or action. For Paul, love is not so much a food as a condiment which gives food a certain taste! Two people can say exactly the same thing, do exactly the same action, make exactly the same gesture to another, but because one acts and speaks lovingly and the other does not, the two are poles apart.

"Send your Holy Spirit and pour into our hearts that most excellent gift of love." We need to remind ourselves that Paul is writing about love to a community which would have been surprised to be regarded as other than very religious. Corinthian Christians were doing all the right things as well as all the wrong things. They gathered for the Eucharist. Probably the reading of the psalms and the scriptures were of a high order! If they had had a hymn book, it is most likely their choir would have been of first-class quality! But Paul in his wisdom saw that all this was missing the point of true Christian lifestyle and true Christian community. Paul had one single criterion by which he judged this and any other community. Was the basis of their lives and of their life together loving? The terrible fact is that religion can be most sincere, most conscientious, most faithful, most brilliant, most pietistic, and utterly unloving! It is capable of doing and being all the right things for all the wrong reasons. The petitions within this collect, for ourselves and for our Christian community, are a prayer that this may not be so with us and among us! Thanks be to God.

Sunday between 28 August and 3 September, Proper 22

Author and Giver of all good things,
graft in our hearts the love of your name,
increase in us true religion,
nourish us in all goodness,
and of your great mercy keep us in the same;
through Jesus Christ our Lord,
who lives and reigns with you and the Holy Spirit,
one God, now and for ever.

It is said of Queen Elizabeth I that she once remarked that when she died the name of Calais would be found engraved on her heart. It is also said in the prophet Isaiah that God bears the name of his people carved in the hollow of his hand. Again, it is a traditional symbol of romance that two people carve their names or their initials in the bark of a tree, expressing their love for one another. In each case the imprint of the name is seen as a measure of the love that is felt.

"Graft in our hearts the love of your name." Frequently in the collects we are concerned with loving God. What does it mean to love God? We get a hint about this in one of the letters of Saint John. He speaks a great deal about loving God, but at one stage he says very bluntly and realistically that if we cannot love a brother or sister whom we have seen, how can we love God whom we have not seen. In other words, the primary way we love God is through loving God's creation. This is surely quite true. There are moments when one is moved to the depths of one's being by a beautiful scene. As one takes it in, one moves beyond the loveliness of the creation to the creator. One is in that moment loving God. It is possible to be moved to the depths intellectually toward the loving of God. Some of the early scientists of recent centuries, particularly Isaac Newton, were at times filled with such a sense of wonder at the universe they had stumbled into, that they expressed their responses in a wondering love of God. Perhaps farther up the scale of human achievement is a different kind of situation. Someone may be going through an agony because of the suffering or the death of someone they love very much. It is a moment when they have every excuse to question the ways of God, even to wrestle fiercely with God in terms of accepting this event. As they look at their loved one they find themselves suddenly aware of the love they have shared, the blessings they have lived out together over many years, and they find themselves moving toward the love of a God who has been companion through all that time, who gave that mutual love, and who now suffers with them both as they move with this God through the shadowlands of life. Loving God is a most complex and mysterious and strangely beautiful concept.

"Increase in us true religion." We pray this because there are many kinds of religion and many things which masquerade as religion. There can be a great deal of religion which is firmly based on prejudice and hatred. There is much religion which is brimming over with the most sickly sentimentality. There is much religion which uses God and the things of God to manipulate people and to use their feelings and their needs for personal gain. In our own personal life we can use religion to prevent our facing reality, either about ourselves or others. Our prayer here is that our Christian faith may be mature, honest, and realistic.

"Nourish us in all goodness and . . . keep us in the same." A word which has become very much used in recent years is the word "nurture." We are realizing that Christian faith is far from being a body of intellectual knowledge which one gets to know and thus becomes a Christian. We are realizing that Christianity is not so much a matter of being as becoming. Becoming a Christian is a lifelong process in which we constantly need nurturing and, perhaps even more important if we are to be mature people, a life-long process in which we give nurture to others. Our growth in Christ is rather like our growth in any relationship. It does not just happen. It takes work and effort and commitment to "keep us in the same." Thanks be to God.

Sunday between 4 and 10 September, Proper 23

Stir up, O Lord,
the wills of your faithful people,
that richly bearing the fruit of good works,
we may by you be richly rewarded;
through Jesus Christ our Lord,
who is alive and reigns with you and the Holy Spirit,
one God, now and for ever.

One of the very fine hymns of our tradition asks God to breathe upon us until "my heart is pure; Until with thee I will one will, to do and to endure." Apart from being a very beautiful moment of prayer, it is also a salutary reminder that religion is not merely about feelings. Actually the lines of the hymn strike a valuable balance. By mentioning the heart it does not deny that feelings are a necessary and integral part of Christian faith, but by speaking of the will it corrects our illusion that faith is merely emotion.

It is necessary to say this today because we live in a world where the emotional is highly prized and widely used to manipulate us all. The myriad of images on our movie and television screens has brought the art of emotional manipulation to a very high level. The vast world of advertising has invested billions in the analysing of human emotions and responses. Today our understanding of human love is primarily in terms of the emotions, so much so that when the emotion of love passes, it is considered quite reasonable to end the relationship.

The truth is very different in Christian experience. Our relationship with Our Lord begins as does any other relationship. There is something that attracts us. We are drawn by those feelings of attraction. We wish to know more about this person. We may move into a deep commitment to him. All of this can be deeply moving and can probe the full gamut of our feelings. But there will come a time, again as in every other relationship, when feelings pass, emotions die. They must wrestle with time, familiarity, predictability. There may come a time when it may not be attractive or romantic to act in a Christian way in a particular situation. Our Lord himself did not always act in a way which mirrors the cliché stained-glass-window Jesus dispensing gentle pleasantness in all directions! He could be stern, dismissive, challenging. He could make demands of accountability on people. He had to summon all his powers of decision and resilience to pursue the way to which he felt called. All of this takes far more than emotions, although there may be a great deal of exhausting emotion involved. All such things take will, sometimes an implacable will.

"Stir up, O Lord, the wills of your faithful people." It is all too easy to stir up religious emotions. It is very much more difficult to stir up our will. But it is important to do so because we are going through a period of history when being Christian — for that matter, being a believer in any of the great historic spiritualities — takes considerable will if we are not to be swept away in the many extreme emotional streams which flow in them all. We hear Paul warning against this danger in his own day for much the same reason. Religion in New Testament times tended to chose frantic and emotional ways of expression in the face of the frantic and threatening nature of the age. The religious situation in a tense and tumultuous age is rather like that of the person threatened with a frightening disease who will try the most extraordinary medications and treatment.

"Bearing the fruit of good works." A spirituality that has the commitment of our will as well as our feeling issues in our involvement in real ways with other people and the world. Such a spirituality of our will as well as our feeling can remain faithful when things are far from easy. Its rewards? Our more-than-adequate reward is the deep sense of meaning and purpose for our lives which we possess from having such a commitment to Our Lord. Thanks be to God.

Sunday between 11 and 17 September, Proper 24

Almighty God,
you call your Church to witness
that in Christ we are reconciled to you,
Help us so to proclaim the good news of your love,
that all who hear it may turn to you;
through Jesus Christ our Lord,
who lives and reigns with you and the Holy Spirit,
one God, now and for ever.

"Almighty God, you call your church to witness." There is something very important which many Christians forget. The church has a number of roles. One of them is to call society beyond itself and its norms and standards, and to remind society that there is a Lord who calls it to serve his will. Much of the church's preaching is to that end. However, it is demanded of the church that it not merely speak about certain things but, at the very least, show signs of embodying those things in its own ongoing corporate life.

For instance, the church exhorts people to be trusting and open with one another. Is trust and openness possible in its own corporate life? The church exhorts us to reach out in rich and deep relationships. What signs of such relationships are in the life of a parish or a diocese? The church exhorts us to reach from our national affluence to the poor. What evidence is there of this in the financial affairs of the church itself? The church exhorts people to seek justice within our society and in other societies where there is great injustice. Do we see a like justice in the behaviour of the church itself? Do we for instance see it in the church's treatment of its own employees? Thus the church is called to witness. One particular way is mentioned in the collect. The church is called to show "that in Christ we are reconciled to you." What do we mean by that at this particular time in history?

Reconciliation is the opposite of alienation. When there is alienation in a relationship, a community, a congregation, it takes grace to bring about reconciliation. That grace needs to be strong and effective to shift people from deeply entrenched positions, from situations where there are scars from past hurts and arguments.

We live at a time when there is a great deal of alienation. It exists on every level of life and in every institution and community; it exists today deep within the human spirit itself. The world and the time we live in alienate. It is a world caught in massive and mysterious change, and God asks us to live in it as faithfully as possible. But to do so is not easy. Our contemporary experience alienates us from ourselves and from one another. It tears apart communities and institutions. We take up different positions and shout across great gulfs at each other. We label one another, dismiss one another, name one another as the enemy. We fear one another. All of this is present in today's church. It is not only present between different traditions but also within traditions and within congregations.

Yet if the church is to dare exhort the world of our time toward reconciliation rather than alienation, then we Christians "must witness that in Christ we are reconciled," reconciled to the God who is the God of this changing and heaving world we are asked to serve in. We must cease to be alienated to our age and society. That does not in the least mean that we must accept it uncritically. But we must cease resenting our vocation of living through this time. Hamlet cried out, "The time is out of joint; O cursed spite,

that ever I was born to set it right!'' That is classic alienation, from oneself, from others, from one's society, one's
responsibilities, one's world.

When as Christians we become reconciled to our contemporary vocation, we shall then, and only then, be able
"to reclaim the good news of your [God's] Love." Thanks
be to God.

Sunday between 18 and 24 September, Proper 25

Almighty God,
you have created the heavens and the earth,
and ourselves in your image.
Teach us to discern your hand in all your works
and to serve you with reverence and thanksgiving;
who is alive and reigns with you and the Holy Spirit,
one God, now and for ever.

"Almighty God, you have created the heavens and the earth." The word *creation* and other words derived from it have become more and more part of our everyday language in recent years. The reason is the changing relationship between our humanity and the rest of creation. The change in this relationship is one of the great factors in the massive paradigm change through which we are all passing in our lifetime.

Until recently we in the western world saw ourselves as apart from creation. We could do things to it, analyse it, use it, change it, manipulate it, form it, and reform it — all for our purposes. Today we are realizing, sometimes at our great cost, that we and the rest of creation are one and that we must learn to live symbiotically with every other creature which God has made, whether that creature be an invisible piece of genetic material or an ocean thousands of miles wide.

Another great change we are experiencing is the coming of an increasing sense of awe among us. Ironically this arises from our own discoveries in the physical and life sciences, particularly in biology, genetics, mathematics, and physics. The more we discover, the more we are being driven back to the realization of a creator. This theme is recurring today in places and among people who even two decades ago would have laughed the idea out of court.

"You have created . . . ourselves in your image." Nowhere are we facing a greater sense of mystery than in the area of our own humanity. We have learned to do many things with ourselves at every stage of life, from birth to death and much in between. We are now being forced to ask a completely new question. It is facing us in many forms which multiply almost by the month — such is the exponential rate of change. The question is, Should we necessarily do something merely because we have achieved the ability to do it? or Are there some things we can do that we must not do? We are facing our response to the question, What is human? What is essential to our humanity? For instance, does there come a stage in the suffering of a human being in his or her quest for the extension of life, when issues such as dignity and the integrity of our humanity become more important than the application of life-extending procedures? The consequential question also haunts us, Who among us has the right to make these decisions with us and for us?

Such are the challenges that face the present and future of Christian spirituality. There is no source of neat specific answers. But the collect does pray that we do one thing, that we "discern your hand in all your works." The prayer is that we look upon all discovery as a revelation of God to be used according to the love and will of God. No discovery is in itself either good or evil. Only its subsequent use brings one or other value judgement into being. Again, the collect prays that we "Serve you with reverence and thanksgiving." If we do not reverence life, our criterion for its value will become more and more one of function and usefulness. Even that measuring of function and usefulness may come to be made on the brutal basis of such things as our capacity to produce, or even worse, our capacity to consume! We are realizing that only two things stand in the way of such a hellish future. First is the biblical conviction that human beings and all other living things are the creation of a Creator. Second is the Christian conviction that every human being has a unique value and dignity, because human nature has been graced by the indwelling of God through Jesus Christ. Thanks be to God.

Sunday between 25 September and 1 October, Proper 26

Grant, O merciful God,
that your Church,
being gathered by your Holy Spirit into one,
may show forth your power among all peoples,
to the glory of your name;
through Jesus Christ our Lord,
who lives and reigns with you and the Holy Spirit,
one God, now and for ever.

"Grant, O merciful God, that your Church being gathered by your Holy Spirit into one." It would be understandable if we smiled sadly as we heard this petition in worship. It would not be surprising if the word *unrealistic* came to mind.

Earlier in this century there was a great dream among Christians. It was not shared by all but certainly by a majority. It was the ecumenical dream, or the dream of unity. It was quite rightly recognized that the divisions in Christianity have done much to weaken its witness in the world. It was recalled that in his great prayer in the gospel according to John, Our Lord prays intensely and repeatedly that his followers be one. But that dream has faded, at least it has seemed to fade in recent decades. In fact, recently a strange and unforeseen process began. While many of the issues that divided the historic Christian traditions began to fade, other issues arising from the intense and varied spirituality of the times began to divide the traditions within themselves.

The situation today is one of mingled evidence. In some

ways Christians are very divided, and in some ways the most encouraging things are quietly happening. A short list of such promising things may surprise us. There has been a gulf between those who saw Christian evangelism as directed only toward individual conversion and those who saw it in terms of impinging on society and its structures and policies. That gulf is very much narrower, with so-called "liberals" and so called "evangelicals" finding themselves on common ground. There has been a gulf between those who saw moral issues only in terms of individual and family life and those who saw moral issues in terms of society and international affairs. That gulf is narrowing with the growing recognition that it must be both.

There is a third element in Christian experience today which has brought about a quiet revolution. On the surface it may sound academic, but it may yet be seen as the most significant growing together in late twentieth-century Christian life. The forming of a Common Lectionary, even with some variations in different traditions, has brought millions of Christians to read and reflect on the same three passages of scripture on Sunday morning. That fact cannot be without a deep cumulative effect on the unity of Christians, and is certainly part of the operation of the Holy Spirit in these days.

"That your church... may show forth your power among all peoples to the glory of your name." This petition is not a prayer for institutional power. We are not asking for the means to flex Christian muscles in society, although that temptation is present in various areas of the world, particularly in elements of American religious life. The prayer is not merely for sociopolitical power. It is a prayer that the life of the Christian churches may become imbued with a spirituality which will give Christian faith an integrity and attractiveness which will draw men and women to it, as they search for meaning in this present age. The power the collect would have us pray for is the kind of spiritual power which brings glory to the name of God as known to us in Jesus Christ. Thanks be to God.

Sunday between 2 and 8 October, Proper 27

Almighty God,
you have built your Church
on the foundation of the apostles and prophets,
Jesus Christ himself being the chief cornerstone.
Join us together in unity of spirit by their teaching,
that we may become a holy temple, acceptable to you;
through Jesus Christ our Lord,
who lives and reigns with you and the Holy Spirit,
one God, now and for ever.

"Almighty God, you have built your church." Very often we Christians make the mistake of thinking of the church building as the church. When we do this we need to be reminded that the church building is merely the place in which the church meets. In its most ancient and genuine sense the church is the body of those who gather together. The Greek word *ecclesia*, from which we get the English word *church* does not stand for a building but for a people gathered together.

All of this may seem obvious and repetitive, but it needs to be said often, because the temptation to make the church building the heart of the church is very strong. Perhaps there is a reason in our past, something that affected the way people have ever since thought about the church. We get an echo of it in this collect.

Saint Paul, writing a letter to a Christian community in Ephesus, begins to speak about Christians as being together the body of Christ. But the images he uses are that of a building. He speaks of "building" and "joints." We get the same links between Our Lord's body and an actual building when Our Lord speaks of rebuilding the temple in three days. The gospel writer assures us that Jesus was referring to his own body. However, in many such ways the link is made that will always be instinctive and strong. For many committed and sincere Christians the building can itself become the body of Christ, to an extent far greater than they themselves realize. If that happens, such a person can go through agony when any change to the building becomes necessary because of the changing nature of worship and church life. Add to this the centuries of tradition about the sanctuary being the place where the body of Christ is sacramentally reserved in the tabernacle, and the association between the body of Christ and the actual church building is even stronger.

"The foundation of the apostles and prophets." Even though much of the language of this collect uses images of building, it points us away from physical buildings. By referring to these apostles and prophets as being the "foundation" of the church, we mean that their lives and witness, their thought and teaching, their suffering and sacrifice are what the church is founded upon. Not only this, but such commitment on the part of each generation will always be the foundation of the people of God.

"Jesus Christ himself being the chief cornerstone." Referring to Our Lord in this way drives home what we will always mean by any images of building. The foundation stone of the Christian church is a person, a life lived, a sacrifice made, a triumph achieved.

"Join us together in unity of Spirit by their teaching." That must always be the only way that building takes place — the building of people in their inner selves and the bonding of those people to one another to form a people of God. All other building comes later and is less important. Only in this way do Christians "become a holy temple." Notice that we do not primarily build a holy temple. We become a holy temple. When that happens — and it is never completely finished — we may or may not build a temple to meet in. But that temple is not the church. It is the place where the church meets. This needs to be said a thousand times if we are to be faithful to Our Lord, our true and only foundation and cornerstone. Thanks be to God.

Sunday between 9 and 15 October, Proper 28

Almighty God,
in our baptism you adopted us for your own.
Quicken, we pray, your Spirit within us,
that we, being renewed both in body and mind,
may worship you in sincerity and truth;
through Jesus Christ our Lord,
who lives and reigns with you and the Holy Spirit,
one God, now and for ever.

"Almighty God, in our baptism you adopted us for your own." There is something lovely and gentle about the sound of the words *for your own*. We might quietly and simply reflect on what is being said about each one of us as Christians.

We belong to God. We know who we are in a world and time when millions do not. We have been found when there is a terrible sense of lostness. Our lives have been given meaning when there is a desperate sense of meaninglessness. All of those things are true because of our baptism. Perhaps this is a good moment to remember what is said about baptism in the Prayer Book catechism. In baptism we are made a member of Christ, the child of God, and an inheritor of the kingdom of heaven. Once again, in a different way but expressing the same glorious truths, we are being told who we are and whose we are.

But only if we understand the depths of the mystery of our baptism will we ever realize these things. Today baptism is returning into the communal life and worship of the church. The baptism of adults is becoming more and more familiar. It is significant that whenever an adult presents him or herself for baptism in front of the congregation, there are always those who will afterward confess themselves to have been deeply moved by the sight. It awakes depths of meaning about the mystery and power of baptism that have never been realized, because it has been understood by so many of us as a far-away event in childhood.

In baptism we are adopted by God. All of us are aware of the need that sometimes comes to a person who has been adopted. No matter how wonderful the mutual love has been in the adoptive family, there may come a time when the adopted child, now no longer a child, feels compelled to trace and meet his or her parent. The desire and the process can be painful, yet many times it results in a deep contentment for all concerned.

In our spiritual experience the position is reversed. We may know our actual parents, but we must now set out on a journey to encounter the one who adopted us in baptism. For a Christian that journey is the lifelong search for the full truth and beauty and holiness of Our Lord. He is the one through whom our adoption has taken place. His is the face that, to the extent we can trace it, allows us to see in turn the face of God who has adopted us for his own.

"Quicken, we pray, your Spirit within us." For what purpose? To send us on the journey in search of the meaning of our own baptism. Why is this important? Because only when we know the meaning of our baptism, do we know truly who we are. This cannot be emphasised too much. Not until a man or woman looks in the mirror, either literally or metaphorically, and sees the cross of their baptism on their forehead, do they know who they are spiritually. When they do know, they find themselves "renewed both in body and mind."

How is that renewal acted out ? In what ways does a quickened spirit show itself? In "worship in sincerity and truth." Why worship? Because worship is to our relationship with God what making love is in a human relationship. Worship is the activity in which we show our intentionality about our relationship with God through Our Lord. The simple truth is that baptism lies in us Christians rather like an unexploded bomb, a bomb with a difference. When it explodes it means renewal, new life, transformation. Thanks be to God.

Sunday between 16 and 22 October, Proper 29

Almighty and everliving God,
increase in us your gift of faith,
that forsaking what lies behind
and reaching out to what is before,
we may run the way of your commandments
and win the crown of everlasting joy;
through Jesus Christ our Lord,
who lives and reigns with you and the Holy Spirit,
one God, now and for ever.

Somehow it is hard to imagine Saint Paul taking time off. We get the impression of a person unrelentingly serious, driven, singleminded. That may be unfair. He must have had moments when the task was put off for a while. One searches for that possibility because there is a theme which occurs frequently in his images — that of the races in the sports stadium. If one can imagine Paul accepting an invitation anywhere to relax and enjoy life, it is to the games. He was fond of seeing life in terms of these races, especially Christian life. It sounds here in this collect.

"Increase in us your gift of faith." How easily we forget the reality of our spiritual situation. It takes a statement like this to make us realize that even the faith we already have is itself the gift of God. We sometimes think we have given God something by our turning and believing and following and worshipping. We find it difficult to realize that all of that is not our gift bestowed generously on a deserving God, but God's gift to us! We have to first receive the gift of faith from God before we offer it back. So how do we increase that faith? We cannot. Its source is God. Therefore we cannot turn on more faith, as we would reach for a tap in our own lives to increase the flow. The only way to increase our faith is to ask the source of faith for its increase.

"Forsaking what lies behind and reaching out to what is before." Here is another image of the races. If there is a golden rule in races, it is that one does not look back. A very famous incident in the history of the one-mile race occurred when John Landry and Roger Bannister were wrestling for victory in Vancouver in 1954, for what was to become the world's first under-four-minute mile. Immediately before the end, Landry, who was slightly ahead, looked back. Just as he did so, Bannister passed him on the other side to win. Such a moment becomes a parable of our life journey. This attitude is very obvious all through the Bible in the journey of the people of God. In the wilderness Moses is always trying to get his people to see that they must not look back nostalgically toward Egypt. They must look forward to the future land. In the gospel itself there is Our Lord's warning about putting one's hand to the plough and turning back. After the resurrection there is the news to those who return to the tomb that the Lord cannot be found by coming back to this place. He has gone before them. He is ahead. That is to be the direction of their lives.

So with us, Christian faith points ahead, not back. In this matter Christian faith is immensely healthy and creative and positive. There may be things behind us that we wish were not there, things we wish had not been done or said, things we need to receive forgiveness for and to forgive ourselves for. But they are past, behind, gone. If we have genuinely confessed them to God and to ourselves, if we have received forgiveness for them, which we certainly have if we prayed for it, then we leave them behind. We do not look back. In fact, we begin to do the exact opposite. We reach out ahead. That becomes the direction of our attention and our energies.

''And win the crown of everlasting joy.'' The goal of life for a Christian is to journey toward Jesus Christ. But that does not mean that Our Lord is waiting for our earthly lives to end before we encounter him. Nothing could be further from the truth. For a Christian the running of the race is to have the companionship of Our Lord in the race itself. Here we discover a paradoxical truth, hard to explain but experienced by so many as to be undeniable. To run the race, or to live life, with the felt and experienced companionship of Our Lord, is to have already won. Thanks be to God.

Sunday between 23 and 29 October, Proper 30

Lord God our redeemer,
who heard the cry of your people
and sent your servant Moses
to lead them out of slavery,
free us from the tyranny of sin and death,
and by the leading of your Spirit
bring us to our promised land;
through Jesus Christ our Lord,
who lives and reigns with you and the Holy Spirit,
one God, now and for ever.

Christians sometimes become disturbed if they hear a person referring to some aspect of the faith as a myth. It seems to be relegating faith to the same level as fairy tale or legend. But while that can be true, it is not necessarily true. Sometimes when the word *myth* is used, it is not in the least denying or doubting that the event in question is very much rooted in reality. The term *myth* indicates that the meaning of the event can be grasped on many levels. We have an example of such an event in the part of scripture on which this collect is based.

"Lord God our redeemer, who heard the cry of your people and sent your servant Moses to lead them out of slavery." Here in a line or two is the heart of one of the world's great historical events, also one of the world's great stories. But as with all great Bible stories, it is not enough for us to receive it merely as an interesting past event. Here is where the use of the word *myth* comes in. We might ask ourselves why there is such staying power in this story, why it can be used as the basis of a prayer in a society existing thirty-four centuries after the event?

To say that the meaning of this long-ago event has deep meaning for us today, and will have for the human situation till the end of time, is to claim that it is a mythic event. There are truths in it about human experience which are universals, true in every place and time. To see this we have only to look at the main outline of the Exodus story.

The people of God are in slavery in Egypt. God sends to them a leader whose name is Moses. This man wrestles with the king for their freedom. Eventually they gain release, but at great cost and in great danger. They are pursued by the Egyptians. They find themselves between the army and the sea. They choose to risk themselves to the sea and it parts for them, returning to drown their enemies. They move from there into a bleak, inhospitable wilderness where they must work very hard to survive, both physically and spiritually. They come to Mount Sinai where they encounter the power and majesty and law of God in a new way. The journey continues toward a new land but is still very far from complete. That is the past event. But every aspect of the event is true within our own lives.

''Free us from the tyranny of sin and death, and by the leading of your Spirit bring us to our promised land.'' All of us are called by God to move from the familiar, the given, the safe, the place where we have been for some time, whether it be in childhood or at any stage of our lives. We cannot stay in our ''Egypt.'' To give us the drive to make the break or the change, we need someone to come from beyond ourselves. We need a grace given to us by God's Holy Spirit. That is our ''Moses.'' To make the break for our ''freedom'' is very costly. The struggle is painful, sometimes against parts of ourselves, sometimes against those who care for us and love us. At first we are fragile and still in danger. Many ''armies'' attack us, armies of doubt and anxiety and guilt and fear and nostalgia. To survive those armies we have to make an act or acts of great trust, trust in ourselves, in others, in God. Such times are our crossing of the ''Red Sea.'' From there we must pass through a "wilderness" in our lives. It can be lonely and frightening and dangerous. Within that wilderness journey we will seek to come to an encounter with God which is renewing and grace-giving. That is our "Sinai" encounter, and there may well be more than one. Such encounters give us the grace to seek our "new land," our future stage, where we continue to serve and worship and work and grow. Thanks be to God.

Sunday between 30 October and 5 November, Proper 31

Almighty God,
Whose chosen servant Abraham obeyed your call,
rejoicing in your promise
that in him the family of the earth is blessed,
give us faith like his,
that in us your promises may be fulfilled;
through Jesus Christ our Lord,
who lives and reigns with you and the Holy Spirit,
one God, now and for ever.

Once again we have a collect which is formed out of a great past reality, in this case a great life, that of Abraham. Once again we are made to realize that across the millenia this past event still speaks and teaches. What does it teach?

"Almighty God, whose chosen servant Abraham obeyed your call." The first level on which we are being addressed tells us two things about this long-ago man. God called him and he obeyed the call. From that obedience a whole history flowed, a whole people were born, and God was given an instrument through which to work the divine will in history. Abraham himself was never to know the full consequences of his obedience.

But the second level on which this statement in the collect speaks to us is on the level of our lives. That Abraham was chosen by God is important, but it is just as important that each one of us is potentially a chosen person! We ask how? By our Christian baptism. What are we chosen for?

To be a servant of God in the world of our time. However, we must carefully note that God's choosing of us does not make us God's servant. We do not become God's servant until we do what Abraham did. Abraham obeyed God's call. So must we. Only then do we become the servant of God. Only then do we become an instrument of God's will in the world.

In the relationship between a Christian and his or her Lord there is a single word which is all-important. The word is yes, yes to God. The irony and the wonder is that the moment we have said yes to God, we find that we have also said yes to our own deepest and finest being.

"Abraham obeyed your call, rejoicing in your promise." What enabled Abraham to say his yes to God was that he trusted God. Most of us find trusting difficult, whether we are talking about trusting others, trusting ourselves, or trusting God. We need to examine the pattern of our relationships with ourselves and with others. Is trust difficult for us in our ongoing lives? If it is, then it will be even more difficult to trust God. Yet it is our lack of trust which will limit God's use of us. One of the pieces of spiritual work we may need to do is to offer God a steady stream of prayer that we may be given the spiritual gift of trust. We would be praying for that gift not merely for our own self-improvement but so that we may be more useful servants for God.

Notice the significance of the word *promise*. Abraham obeyed while "rejoicing in God's promise." A promise is not a guarantee. A promise needs a greater response of trust than a guarantee. We receive a guarantee with relief and gratitude. We trust a promise with excitement and anticipation. We want guarantees from God, but we are given promises. We are actually a people of promise.

"Give us faith like his, that in us your promises may be fulfilled." The collect now makes explicit what we have been thinking about. The whole point of scripture is that it be not only a recalling but a reliving. Abraham was called.

We are called. Abraham said yes. How can we become believers in God's promise for this time in history, a time when millions see no promise but merely threat? Notice how the collect prays that in us God's promises may be fulfilled. God needs the existence of a people to receive the promises, to trust them, and to live them. We are so called. Thanks be to God.

Sunday between 6 and 12 November, Proper 32

Eternal God,
who caused all holy scriptures
to be written for our learning,
grant us so to hear them,
read, mark, learn, and inwardly digest them,
that we may embrace and ever hold fast
the blessed hope of everlasting life,
which you have given us in our Saviour Jesus Christ,
who lives and reigns with you and the Holy Spirit,
one God, for ever and ever.

After an English monarch is crowned, the archbishop comes forward, places a Bible in the newly crowned monarch's hands, and says, "Here is the most precious thing this world affords. Here is truth. Here is the royal law. These are the lively oracles of God." It may well be the loveliest description and the most majestic tribute paid to holy scripture.

Scripture is one of the great gifts of God to his people. As Christians we inherited some scriptures and we wrote others. We inherited our first scriptures from God's older people. Then, in our efforts to express for our common life the meaning of the life, death, and resurrection of Our Lord, we wrote further scriptures for the Christian community. Both sets of scriptures grew out of our human understanding of God's dealings with us. We also believe and trust that in the writing of these scriptures God's Holy Spirit guided and responded to our groping efforts. That is something of what we mean when we say that "God caused all holy scriptures to be written for our learning."

"Grant us to hear them, read, mark, learn, and inwardly digest." The sequence asks for our deeper and deeper involvement and commitment. We can read something and still remain totally outside it. We can say, "How interesting," and pass along our way unaffected. What the collect prays is for us to allow scripture to enter into us. It is significant that we describe our response to scripture and the bread of Eucharist with the same word. We *digest* both, thus in a sense making scripture sacramental. Why digest these writings? Why make them an integral part of our lives? Because they contain a "blessed hope of everlasting life."

We human beings are always in search of something to replace a lostness within us. In both the Old and New Testaments the Bible puts a finger on this sadness and lostness. Genesis tells us how we lost, and how each one of us loses, our close relationship with God. We "fall" away from it, pushed by the fascination we feel for our own self-will and the things of the world. Our Lord also tells us that there is a kingdom within ourselves from which we are exiles. We are shut out of that kingdom of God by that same self-fascination which blinds us. We get glimpses but no more. Actually we saw that kingdom with terrible and fascinating clarity in Our Lord's own life, and our response was to kill him! Thus we discovered that there is something inside us that is not only exiled from the kingdom of God but is really the enemy of the kingdom!

That is our human predicament. The Bible calls it sin. At worst it can breed a hopelessness about ourselves. We very badly need a compensating hope. That hope throbs and sings and calls throughout scripture. The collect is praying that we may hear the music of that great and living and loving hope.

All through scripture that hope is offered to us in the willingness of a loving God to remain in covenant with us no matter what we do. Nothing breaks the love of God.

Our Lord is the climax of that hope. If our humanity holds within its flawed and sinful nature the glory which we see in Jesus, then there is hope. If a man or woman embraces that hope, it can make all the difference in his or her living of life. Thanks be to God.

Sunday between 13 and 19 November, Proper 33

Almighty God,
you sent your Son Jesus Christ
to be the light of the world.
Free us from all that darkens and ensnares us,
and bring us to eternal light and joy;
through the power of him
who is alive and reigns with you and the Holy Spirit,
one God, now and for ever.

Light is one of the most powerful elements in our lives. I can remember a friend whose job it was to visit the communities of armed forces stationed along the Distant Early Warning line in the far north. All were living at a latitude which gave them six months of light and six months of near darkness. Each of my friend's two annual visits was made in those different periods. He said it was like being in two different communities. To visit in the long darkness was to find angers, depressions, anxieties, arguments, psychosomatic illnesses. To visit in the long period of light was to find joyousness, joking, energy, good relationships, health.

This is only one example of the power of light as a symbol of our lives. It is not for nothing that the sun hung in the heavens for millennia as a god for our human need. But all through Christian history light has been used as a metaphor for Our Lord and his life and work among us.

What is that which "darkens and ensnares us"? In asking the question we are facing once again that sadness and lostness which scripture calls sin, of which we spoke in the previous reflection. At that time we used the images of hope both lost and rediscovered in scripture. Now we use images of darkness and light.

Our darkness is within our deepest self, in the depths of our human nature. God did not fashion us with that darkness. Saint John tells us in the Bible that in God there is no darkness at all. But each of us chooses to extinguish the light of God within us, preferring our own source of light. It takes us a while in life to realize that our own kind of light is really a kind of darkness where we can get very lost. We need another light, certainly one other than our self. Jesus Our Lord offers himself as that other source of light.

I can recall deciding to go through the long darkness of Hezekiah's rock tunnel in Jerusalem with three friends. At the entrance someone offered us a strong light, saying that we would need it. We refused it, choosing instead to depend on a weak small pocket light which one of us happened to have. We regretted that decision in the darkness and the water of the tunnel, and we had a worrying and frightening time. We emerged safely, but we had greatly wished for that other light.

This is a parable of our life's journey and its spiritual path. As Christians we have had the immense good fortune to have been offered a source of light outside ourselves. Using the phrase "outside ourselves" needs some correction. The source of our spiritual light does not lie outside us in the sense of being in past history. Jesus *was* the light, but the Risen Christ *is* our light. The light is now and is available to us now. Neither is the light outside us in the sense of being outside our human nature. The light is in us for us to find because Christ, who is the light, is in us by our baptism! The kingdom, the light, the Holy Spirit, Christ himself is within us. We cannot emphasize that too often, and we cannot give thanks for that too often.

To possess the light of Christ is to taste a kind of freedom. It is the freedom we get when a light is suddenly ignited in darkness. Instead of stumbling and groping and falling, we are free to walk with confidence and purpose. As the collect says, with the coming of light comes joy. Thanks be to God.

The Last Sunday after Pentecost: the Reign of Christ, Proper 34

Almighty and everlasting God,
whose will it is to restore all things
in your well-beloved Son, our Lord and King,
grant that the peoples of the earth,
now divided and enslaved by sin,
may be freed and brought together
under his gentle and loving rule;
who lives and reigns with you and the Holy Spirit,
one God, now and for ever.

On the eighth of May in the year 1373 a woman had a vision. Her name was Julian. She was what those days called an anchoress, living alone in her cell beside the church in the city of Norwich. In her dream she held in her hand a hazelnut. She asked God what it meant, and God replied that it was all that is made, that God was its Maker and its Lover and its Keeper, and that "all shall be well. All would be well; and all manner of thing shall be well."

"Almighty and everlasting God, whose will it is to restore all things." The collect of this day is echoing that great hope of humanity and great promise of God — that all will be well. This collect is certainly among the most majestic of all the collects. It paints on the largest canvas imaginable, that of all human history and all humanity. In its magnificent first statement there is a hint of tragedy. If all things need to be restored, it means that all things have been damaged in some way. That fact is one of the great themes of scripture. The world is not as it was created to be. Humanity is not as it was created to be. You and I are not as we were created to be. To say that is not to belittle the value of the world or the human in any way. It is to do the very opposite. As G.K. Chesterton once said, ''The doctrine of original sin is also the doctrine of original blessing.'' To say that humanity and society and the whole created order is not what it was created to be, is to give a great cry of hope. If it once was more than it is, then with the grace of God both it and we can be again what we are created to be!

Where is the focus of that hope? Where is it glimpsed through all the shadows of sin, treachery, and pollution which characterize our lives, our race, our societies, and our planet? The collect tells us that it is ''in your well-beloved Son, our Lord and King.''

To understand what is being said here is to grasp the heart of Christian faith. In Jesus Christ we glimpse the realizing of the future hope which we grope and strive for. What is the nature of that hope? The gulf between human will obedient only to itself and human will obedient to the will of God needs to be bridged. To achieve that bridging is to achieve the transformation of human nature, thus to achieve the transformation of human society, and with it the transformation of the relationship between humanity and the created order.

This is the vision which we glimpsed in the life, death, and resurrection of Our Lord Jesus Christ. In the gospel we find in him the transformation of our human nature. We find in him what human nature becomes if it is lived completely in step with the will of God. Later, through the genius of John, we see in Revelation a vision of transformed human society and transformed creation in the description of the Holy City, a society where the rule of God is supreme. Here in this Holy City, over which the Christ who was born among us now rules, we see the prayer of this collect come true. Here in this city all the divisions of humanity have been healed. Those under oppression have been freed.

Human will on its own no longer rules. Christ rules through a transformed human nature. That is the Christian vision. That it will not be fulfilled in time and history does not mean that we refuse our Christian vocation to work and to pray for its coming. This collect is in effect the charter of our Christian calling. Thanks be to God.

Other Books by Herbert O'Driscoll

Child of Peace,Lord of Life : Reflections on the Readings of the Common Lectionary

Year A, Volume 1 (from the First Sunday of Advent to the Fifth Sunday in Lent)

Volume 2 (from the Sunday of the Passion to the Last Sunday after Pentecost)

Year B, Volume 1

Year B, Volume 2

Year C, Volume 1

Year C, Volume 2

A Certain Life: Contemporary Meditations on the Way of Christ

Portrait of a Woman: Meditations on the Mother of Our Lord

Crossroads: Times of Decision for the People of God

The Sacred Mirror: Meeting God in Scripture

One Man's Journal: Reflections in Contemporary Living

City Priest, City People: One Man's Journal, Book 2

Books on Spirituality

Soft Bodies in a Hard World: Spirituality for the Vulnerable *by Charles Davis*

Christ Mind, Zen Mind, Child Mind: A Reflection on Zen and Christian Faith and Practice *by John King*

Books on Christian Life

New Life: Addressing Change in the Church *by JohnBothwell, John Davis, J.C. Fricker, Sheila and George Grant, Dorothy Gregson, Philip Jefferson, Elizabeth Kilbourn*

Light From the East: A Symposium on the Oriental Orthodox and Assyrian Churches *edited by Henry Hill*

Books on Church History

By Grace Co-Wokers: Building the Anglican Diocese of Toronto 1780 — 1989 *edited by Alan L. Hayes*

Frontiers Then and Now: The Canadian Anglican Episcopate 1787 — 1987 *by John A. Baycroft, John M. Flynn, Michael G. Peers, Henry Roper, Edward W. Scott*